Listenable

ENDORSEMENTS

"No matter how good you are at marketing, your long-term success in podcasting will depend on the quality of your content and delivery."

—**John Lee Dumas**, author of *The Common Path to Uncommon Success* and founder & host of *Entrepreneurs On Fire* and *Podcasters' Paradise*

"Getting people to listen to your podcast can take a lot of work. If your content and delivery don't pull listeners in and get them to hit that subscribe button, you will make your life a lot harder than it needs to be. In *Listenable*, Bert Weiss shares a simple system for creating a show that helps you consistently attract the right listeners and keep them around for the long term."

—**Chris Krimitsos**, author of *Start Ugly*, and founder of the Guinness World Record setting podcasting and multi-media conference, *Podfest*

"I've worked with thousands of podcast hosts since I started Interview Valet in 2015 to help match top podcasters with high quality guests looking to grow their business using podcast interview marketing. Since that time, many technologies and podcast growth tactics have come and gone but two podcasting success factors have remained the same: content and delivery. For a host to build a large, loyal audience and a guest to make a genuine connection with listeners, they need to come to the mic with top-quality content delivered in a way that makes it easy for listeners. In *Listenable*, Bert Weiss breaks down simple content and delivery strategies that have stood the test of time and will not go away with the next hot technology or algorithm update."

—**Tom Schwab**, author of Podcast *Guest Profits* and founder of Interview Valet, a concierge-level podcast guest marketing service.

LISTENABLE

The Content and Delivery System
to Set Your Podcast Apart

BERT WEISS

PANTA
PRESS
A BRANDED IMPRINT
OF MORGAN JAMES

NEW YORK

LONDON • NASHVILLE • MELBOURNE • VANCOUVER

LISTENABLE

The Content and Delivery System to Set Your Podcast Apart

Published in New York, New York, by Morgan James Publishing in partnership with Panta Press. Morgan James is a trademark of Morgan James, LLC.
www.MorganJamesPublishing.com

Proudly distributed by Ingram Publisher Services.

A **FREE** ebook edition is available for you
or a friend with the purchase of this print book.

_____

CLEARLY SIGN YOUR NAME ABOVE

Instructions to claim your free ebook edition:
1. Visit MorganJamesBOGO.com
2. Sign your name CLEARLY in the space above
3. Complete the form and submit a photo of this entire page
4. You or your friend can download the ebook to your preferred device

ISBN 9781636980096 paperback
ISBN 9781636980102 ebook
Library of Congress Control Number:
2022945636

Cover Design by:
John Stapleton

Interior Design by:
Chris Treccani
www.3dogcreative.net

Morgan James is a proud partner of Habitat for Humanity Peninsula and Greater Williamsburg. Partners in building since 2006.

Get involved today! Visit MorganJamesPublishing.com/giving-back

CONTENTS

FOREWORD

In 2001, I was the program director of Q100 in Atlanta and an architect for the Blessed Media Event—known as the "Birth of *The Bert Show*." I went on to work for MTV Networks as president of the CMT channel for seventeen years before returning to radio and podcasting at Bert's new radio home, Cumulus Media, in 2019. My job at MTV Networks honed my skills at casting shows, developing scripts, and imagining unforeseen twists in shows, films, and music. Television and radio have each fueled my lifelong love of creative risk-taking. We produced series, big music events, TV movies, and Academy Award–winning theatrical releases.

One of the great pleasures of my return to radio was discovering all Bert and the show had accomplished in my absence. I remembered Bert and accomplices as nervous, hyperactive kids, suddenly thrust onto Atlanta radio's big stage. In the interim, they—and the cast members who came after them—blossomed into Atlanta's "morning-show-of-record." This was four and a half daily hours packed with indelible characters. They were authentic, infinitely curious about other humans, honest, and vulnerable. These are characteristics which, in my experience, in every medium, are always precursors of success and longevity. Bert Weiss and *The Bert Show* have won the hard-earned love of millions.

The attributes that propel smash TV hits, long-running morning radio institutions, big films, and winning podcasts come from the same place.

They are interchangeable. The podcast landscape is the wild frontier, exploding with possibility, yet ever more crowded with entrants. Some podcasters, like Bert, with six million downloads a month, have conquered podcasting, while others fearfully struggle to "decode" this new audio world.

Mass entertainment arrived on the scene in the 1920s with the advent of "radio plays," comedy shows, and live big band concerts. Free entertainment crackled into the living rooms of those suffering through the American Depression. The nature of entertainment never changes. It is *storytelling*—built on human drama, humor, and legend. Yes, it shifts quickly to new format models and platforms. It embraces new technology, tone, and aesthetics. But now, armed with Bert's experience and ability to teach in these fields, you will have a distinct advantage.

With Bert as your guide, you need have no fear. You are on the "inside" of the audio content juggernaut now. Each new era in audio has brought seismic change in audience expectations, business models, and new opportunities for the next generation of people with bold, lucrative new ideas. That's you!

In a universe of more than two million podcasts, you'll need to stand out in distinctive ways and market yourself cleverly to get noticed. As you have no doubt observed, these are Bert's gifts, which he happily shares with each of us in this book. Have a great time mastering the Art of the Perfect Podcast. I leave you in good hands!

—**Brian Philips**, Head of Content and Audience, Cumulus Media

INTRODUCTION:

Read This Book or Die Lonely!

There is *great* news and *bad* news when it comes to podcasting.

The great news? *Anybody* can start a podcast.

The bad news? *Anybody* can start a podcast.

As you know, there are so many incredibly gifted podcasters. After all, you're aiming to be one of them if you're reading this book. As of August 2021, research shows that there are more than two million podcasts and forty-eight million-plus episodes.[1] That's a whole lot of people pumping out content.

---

1 PodcastHosting.org, "2021 Global Podcast Statistics, Demographics & Habits," PodcastHosting.org, April 10, 2021, https://podcasthosting. org/podcast-statistics/.

But the bulk of podcasters have no entertainment or broadcasting background. Which, again, is a blessing and a curse. The blessing? No bad habits picked up from other mediums. The curse? Their podcasts are missing the basics to make them successful, connect, stand out, and make money.

Imagine walking onto the set of a TV show with zero experience and yelling to the crew: "Okay. Roll cameras. I got this." Or a movie set: "Yo, DiCaprio, get out of my shot. This is my first day on set and I don't want you screwing things up for me."

It sounds ridiculous, but hundreds, if not thousands, of so-called podcasters are doing exactly this every day.

I get it. The beauty of podcasting is the freedom and space. And I'm not a rules guy. I hate rules. But we need to cover some basics if you're going to connect with your listeners so they *love* you. And that's the key—connecting. You don't want to be *liked*. You want to be *loved*. You want your audience to be annoyed if your episode is late because they've been waiting for it all week. The loyalty and moneymaking opportunities come when your audience *loves* you. There are too many podcasts to just be "liked." "Liked" is the friend zone.

Loved. That's where we're going to get you.

Who Am I and How Have I Been Gifted with So Much Knowledge?

This book shares observations of successful podcasters including Joe Rogan, Dax Shepherd, and many others. My story, though, stays pretty short because, frankly, I'm sick of me. I've talked about myself for an entire career in morning radio. "*Morning radio?*" you might say in a condescending tone. But the principles of producing a personality-driven morning show are only slightly different from effectively delivering a podcast.

Let's sidebar here for a second. There seems to be an elitist divide between podcasters and radio personalities: "Radio is *soooooooo* limiting and old school." "Podcasters are a bunch of amateurs who have no idea what they are doing." Both are somewhat true. But, honestly, there is *zero* difference between the principles behind personality radio and the principles behind a strong podcast that truly connects with its audience. A Gen Zer said to me, "Radio feels like cable TV while podcasting feels like Netflix." True.

But content is content, and this book is going to walk you through the steps of creating quality content so listeners will want to binge-listen to every single episode as if it were a Netflix series. There's a reason the cliché "content is king" is true. But two podcasters delivering the same material can be vastly different. One delivers content. The other one *feels and connects* the content to the audience.

When I launched my podcasting consultancy, I needed a few case studies. In other words, I was leveraging my morning radio career to move into the podcasting space. So I reached out to a woman who had a strong concept for a podcast, but it needed some tweaks to be even better. I offered free consulting. She essentially said: "You know radio and I respect that. But you don't really know anything about podcasting. So thanks, but no thanks. We kick butt already." (Which they do, by the way.) It was my first potential consultancy, and she punched me right in my ego.

That's when I fully realized that podcasters and radio broadcasters don't want to acknowledge that the talent, formats, and scheduling are the same for both. My radio show is repurposed for a podcast, and it gets more than six million downloads a month as I write this. What does that say? It says the content, material, and delivery are transferable.

What Can You Expect from This Book?

You can expect this book to transform your life. Seriously. You can also expect the book to transform the lives of your listeners. Because with the lessons I'm sharing, you'll be able to start a top-notch podcast from the ground up, avoiding the mistakes so many podcasters are still trying to untangle. We'll talk about the possibilities of podcasting before discussing how to build a loyal audience (which will later turn into a cult following), and how to make any uncomfortable parts of podcasting completely comfortable. I'll then walk you through the pros and cons of having co-hosts; building show schedules; and interview secrets. You'll also learn how to outsource—a no-brainer in the world of podcasting that so many podcasters avoid because of ego, money, or inadequate resources. Trust me, these are all myths. It's time you focused on the whole point of making an impact with your podcast: storytelling.

William Corbin oversees partnerships and revenue for Sound That Brands, one of the top agencies teaching podcasters how to make an impact, and he backs up this belief in the universal power of good storytelling. "One of our partners on the brand side comes from radio, and then became very successful at selling a lot of big podcasts—in the top ten charts at any given time," says Corbin. "He knows how to do it. He knows all the big players, and he knows what makes a compelling audio story, how to script and then how to sell it in."

Content and delivery are priority one for both radio personalities and podcasters. Without excellent content and excellent delivery, you're wasting time, energy, and money. Great storytelling is the key to any form of entertainment, and that goes for radio, TV, podcasting, movies, books, and some dude holding court in the office.

Content + delivery = storytelling.

If you don't buy into this, then you wasted your money on my book. Thanks for the cash. Move on. Nothing to see here.

If this makes sense to you and you read on, I will give you the keys to the kingdom. You will live a complete life of inner peace and contentment full of all the riches in the heavens. People will run 5Ks in your honor. Statues will be erected in your image. Puppies and babies will be named after you. You will never pay for another meal in your city because of your level of fame and no ill should ever befall you.

Too much?

The decision is yours.

Now, Back to Me

Anyway, I didn't search out personality radio. I really wanted to be a sportscaster, so after I got a job in country radio at KSON San Diego, I used the station letterhead and invented my own job title: Sports Director. All the pro leagues gave me press passes, but the backstage access was a complete letdown. Most of the athletes were entitled jerks, and I decided I didn't want to deal with that nonsense my entire life. If anything, I wanted to be the entitled jerk!

So I accidentally slipped into morning radio. The morning guy at the country radio station let me get coffee for him. He put me on the air one morning to talk about some wild party I attended that weekend. It was intoxicating.

From there it was phone screening, producing morning shows, writing, co-hosting, and finally hosting my own syndicated show based out of Atlanta.

That's the short story. The point is I hustled and learned how to do personality-based shows from the ground up. I'm proud to have been inducted into the Georgia Radio Hall of Fame because it shows success over a super long period of time.

During my twenty-year career, I've had a ton of wins and a ton of losses. But I only had success by discovering what *doesn't* work and learning from my mistakes. There are *no* shortcuts except *one*: reading this book and applying everything I tell you.

And I'm passing this on to you because neither of my kids wants anything to do with podcasting. One is an oboe-playing soccer player, and the other is a theater junkie who thinks he's way too good for podcasting. Neither of them cares about my broadcast career, and I'm determined to pass this knowledge on to anyone who will listen.

I do one thing great. Content. I have a dream team of experts I lean on for anything that has to do with podcasting outside of the content. Want to know what's the best mic to use? Heck if I know. But I have the best guy in the podcasting industry who knows, and he's available for you. Want to know the best editing equipment to use for your podcast? You might as well ask me for the meaning of life—I don't know the answer to either of those. But I do know an expert in editing who can help you find the best equipment. (I'm still waiting to find the one who can answer that meaning of life question.). All are important but only *one* makes the others relevant: *content*.

So You're Ready to Start a Podcast Tomorrow?

I mean, technically, yes. You could. But it would probably suck. Like, bad. So let's start working on taking it from sucking enormously to *The Greatest Podcast in the History of Podcasting*.

> You don't want to be *liked*. You want to be *loved*. You want your audience to be annoyed if your episode is late because they've been waiting for it all week. That's where we're going to get you.

You and I are going to be hyper focused on your content, your delivery, your connection, and the sound of your podcast. Without those things, the rest doesn't matter anyway. Why spend time, money, and energy on a podcast that can't retain an audience? An expensive mic will only make your crappy podcast sound crappy with crystal clarity. If your show isn't connecting, you're wasting your time. Content is king! Everything else is secondary. That's your mantra. "Content is king. Content is king."

Podcasting networks are everywhere these days. What's rare is the opportunity to get legitimate talent coaching to maximize your potential.

Welcome to *Listenable*.

The Only Two Things You Really Need for an Amazing Podcast

A super expensive mic that looks shiny and Instagrammable and sounds like I'm speaking right next to you? *No!*

A *humongous* and well-strategized marketing budget that gets your podcast in front of an audience of bazillions, growing exponentially and making Joe Rogan's audience look like a grain of sand on an entire beach! *No.* That is actually ridiculous. You'll waste monstrous amounts of money, lose all your savings, end up homeless and a deep embarrassment to your family.

Once again, the only two things you really need as a foundation for an amazing podcast are

1. Content
2. Delivery

You can spend thousands of dollars on the latest hardware, software, mics, and editing equipment and it won't matter if your content and delivery suck. Why would you want a product that makes your crappy content sound crystal clear? You can find three hundred Ivy League–educated "marketing experts" to help you attract more listeners to your show. But why would you want to attract *one* listener to a show that sucks? In fact, you should hire people to keep listeners away from your show if it sucks. OMG. I just invented a new marketing industry: "How to make sure no one hears my podcast." No money in it, though, 'cause most podcasts are heard once or twice and lose their audience anyway. But not yours!

But together we're going to make sure that doesn't happen. Within these magical pages are the hidden truths of how to create a show that people truly love. I searched the least traveled and darkest corners of the world like Indiana Jones determined to find the lost podcasting scrolls. My sheer grit and dedication took me all the way back to 2004 to selflessly deliver these treasures to you. (Fun fact: one of MTV's original DJs, Adam Curry, is credited with the first podcast).

We're going to build an engaged and loyal audience through a podcast worth promoting far and wide. But you have to commit to following every single rule to the letter or you are destined to fail. (Not true. There is plenty of wiggle room.)

> 78 percent of Americans aged twelve plus are familiar with podcasting[2]
>
> 57 percent of Americans aged twelve plus listen to podcasts[3]
>
> 41 percent of Americans aged twelve plus listen to podcasts monthly
>
> Each week, more Americans listen to podcasts than go to church.[4]

Start Ugly

My first advice to someone who has never been behind a mic is … (ready for this grain of genius?) "Get behind a mic." That's it. Get behind a mic, have a blueprint for ten minutes of content, and start recording. Listen to it. Then delete it because it's really, really bad. Or save it to play back as an outtake when you're good. Do this a few times. Don't shoot for an hour of content. Shoot for five to ten minutes of content and stop! Because you don't want more than ten minutes of this travesty. It really is to just start to

2   Edison Research and Triton Digital, "The Infinite Dial 2021," Triton Digital, March 11, 2021, https://info.tritondigital.com/hubfs/The%20 Infinite%20Dial%202021__FINAL.pdf?.

3   Jay Baer, "Podcast Statistics for 2021 - Charts and Data," Convince & Convert, March 26, 2021, https://www.convinceandconvert.com/ content-marketing/podcast-statistics-charts-and-data/.

4   Statista Research Department, "How Often Do You Attend Church or Synagogue - at Least Once a Week, Almost Every Week, about Once a Month, Seldom, or Never?," Statista, January 24, 2022, https://www. statista.com/statistics/245491/church-attendance-of-americans/.

get used to how you sound and the seeds of what it takes to plan out a show and transition through your content. You will most likely hate your voice. Get over it. In time you'll come to hate it less. Not love it. I've been doing this a long time and *still* hate the sound of my voice.

The founder of Podfest, an annual event that brings together some of the world's top podcasting talent, Chris Krimitsos has one piece of advice for anyone embarking on a new show: start ugly. (It's also the name of his book, which is full of advice about how to stop thinking and start doing.) "The philosophy is not to start ugly and *stay* ugly," he says. "It's to find a balance if you're ready to start. 'Ugly' because every start is ugly compared to where you're going to be, but it starts ugly, and then you perfectly execute from that start with constant, never-ending improvement. It's about constantly improving fractionally every day to create a better product."

So start ugly! Motivational speaker Les Brown says, "Anything worth doing is worth doing badly, until you get it right." He's 100 percent correct: 99 percent of us will start ugly with any new challenge. With experience you get better and more comfortable. So don't be afraid to straight-up suck at first. Don't be defeated. You will suck less each time. I mean, you'll get better each time.

I was helping my friend Dolvett Quince launch his new podcast. Before he even opened a mic, he was asking if the background in his podcast studio would look good on video. He was way ahead of himself. The *only* thing you should be concerned with initially is opening the mic and "starting ugly."

You have creative freedom right now. It's what any creative person wants. And it's precious. Nobody is looking over your shoulder telling you what to do or not to do. You get to pioneer your own way and learn from your own mistakes without *any* pressure.

For a decade I was part of the support staff on morning shows. I finally got hired in Atlanta, stepped into that studio, cracked the mic, and realized I had no idea what I was doing. It was so bad that I actually ran into my program director's office, sat down, and informed him he had made the biggest mistake of his life hiring me. True story. I was *that* freaked out. He said: "Bert, go in the studio, and do whatever you want for the next six weeks. Don't worry about making mistakes. Do the show you've always wanted. We'll meet in six weeks and talk about what's working and what's not."

I looked at him with the same tilted head a dog has when it hears a high pitch. What Brian Philips did for me that day empowered me to fail without consequence. In all my years of entertaining, I never felt so free. Sure, we sucked. But we sucked less every day 'cause I was confident I wasn't going to get fired. My program director understood I had talent. Just no experience. Guess what? You can't teach talent. You're in the same position right now. You have talent. You do have talent, right? All you need is experience. But you have *zero* pressure. Things might change in the future when you create an audience.

But as far as freedom goes, it never gets better than when you first start. Enjoy it!

"Alexa, What's the Best Car?"

From moms, dads, singles, couples, kids and even companies like Audi, Volkswagen, Apple, and even Zoom, it seems like everybody has a podcast these days. It's critical to their marketing campaigns, as William Corbin of Sound That Brands explains. "My biggest fear as a marketer, if I'm working for a client like BMW, is that they don't have a podcast and somebody asks Alexa, 'What's the best car?'" he says. "Alexa might start playing the Audi podcast. It's just like the World Wide Web was in the late nineties. You had to have a website; you just had to put your stake in that space to claim it. Today, if you're not putting a stake in the audio website, which is a podcast, you're going to be behind the eight ball or you're going to get knocked out of the whole space."

Chances are you're reading this book for reasons other than launching a BMW podcast; you've got your own show about DIY car hacks, for example. But getting your "brand," your unique topic, out into the world in the right way is the only way to give it leverage. This book will show you how to have your podcast be the answer to somebody asking Alexa or Siri for knowledge.

Why Read This Book?

Unless you're part of the 0.000001 percent of people who do this instinctively, if you don't read my book and apply what you learn to produce a show that people actually want to listen to you, you are destined to fail at podcasting because the content and delivery will be awful.[5] And when you fail, you self-loathe. And when you self-loathe, people don't want to be around you. And you'll be lonely. Which will force you to isolate and invite stray cats into your home for companionship, but they will eventually try to snack on you as you lie on the floor because your medical alert device didn't notify an ambulance that you were distressed. And this all could have been avoided if you had just read this book and put in place a few small tweaks to make your show listenable.

You Ready?

This is a "how-to guide" for people who hate how-to guides. I despise how-to guides, actually. *Hard yawn.* When I decided I was going to write a helping guide that was strictly focused on the content and delivery of your podcast, I wanted to make sure it was fun. This is no formal, uber-professional podcast bible. I never even learned how to tie my own tie, so let's throw out formality and have a good time making your podcast stand out from the competition.

We're ready to take the next step, right? I've dedicated the first part of this book to sharing the big picture of podcasting: how you connect with your audience, how to

---

5   Yes, 0.000001 percent is a made-up stat. If anything, that's
     overestimating the number of people who do this instinctively …

make money, and how to deal with the sound of your own voice. Then we'll move on to the other people who help make a podcast successful, from a co-host to outsourced editors and consultants (including me). Finally, I'll reveal some interview secrets from the podcasting superstars and give you inside tips on how to addict people to you and your personality.

So let's start working on the most important piece of your podcast: *the thumbnail picture!*

No. Not the thumbnail picture. Not your main logo or website or even social channels.

I'm talking about content and delivery. If all you do well is content and delivery your show will grow and build a cult-like audience.

If you remember two words from this book, make them content and delivery.

Content. Delivery.

Content.

Delivery.

Everything else is secondary.

Let's get this party started!

PART 1:
The Big Picture

CHAPTER 1:

The Possibilities

Meet Tiffany Haynes. In the fall of 2020, she started a podcast called *Permission to Enter* with her best friend, Lauren Chamblin. It was Tiffany's first-ever podcast, dedicated to such topics as wearing crop tops and going to PTA meetings, and "trying to keep our faces hydrated ... and our bodies lubricated." At first, the potential for sharing intimate details of her life intimidated Tiffany, who has a tough time being vulnerable. (Full disclosure: as of this writing, Tiffany and I are engaged to be married.)

So she stretched herself and went for it. And it's opened her up in ways she never saw coming on a few levels.

"A year ago, if you would have asked me to rank my goals and I *had* to include starting a podcast to talk about my personal struggles, it would have been dead last," Tiffany told me as I was writing this book. "Adding up the podcast interviews I had turned down in avoidance of hearing my own introspection, you would confidently bet your last dollar I would never voluntarily be a host of my *own* show."

Once I started to hear Tiffany's story, I had to hear more. So here it is:

I had gifted myself a medal of honor from the war that was my childhood. A medal that granted my conscience permission to take my struggles and vulnerabilities and "neatly" hide them away. They were in a dark room, at the basement level of a beautiful castle, with infinite stories stacked on top of "the chamber" that held what I believed to be poison. Very few could crack the cryptograph to even access the drawbridge to this castle property. Good luck getting past the guarded vestibule and armored door and finding a passage to the room where passage did not exist. Layers and layers of concrete poured around this underground room to ensure its secrets were sealed away for eternity. It would take a nuclear explosion for anything to ever enter or exit the chamber. For those secrets would expose the real truth.

The truth was that I was irreparably damaged, broken beyond repair, and a mere rag doll beaten around by the effects of childhood traumas, sexual abuse, neglect, and everything you could imagine any one human shouldn't ever go through. Ultimately, I felt I was a fatal curse to anyone who was naive enough to believe they may be able to "fix me." I was determined to keep this truth away from my daughter, my family, my friends, and anyone who dare get close enough to be affected by the darkness that lived in me. The ole "out of sight, out of mind" analogy. If I couldn't see it and no one else could see it, it can't be there, right? Wrong. Here's the thing about keeping a real-life lethal poison hidden in a metaphorical room inside a metaphorical castle. The metaphors don't protect your mind, body, soul, or spirit from the slow-leak that occurs when trying to harbor poison. That nuclear explosion is more likely than you ever believed, and your quarantined room has morphed all of the rooms around it into traps of anxiety, guilt, depression, shame, sadness, resentment, and paranoia. Everything is slowly losing color and the poison has grayed everything in its path. Where you eat, where you sleep, and where you live inevitably get infected and there's no safe corner in your own kingdom.

This is what it feels like to bury your past without confronting the emotions and living the experience fully. I wholeheartedly believed I could make it through life while hiding a "truth" deep within me to protect myself and anyone around me. Turns out the real truth was shame had corroded my reality. I believed that because bad things had happened to me, I was bad. And something amazing happened as soon as I made a promise to Lauren Chamblin, my best friend and co-host, that I would do a podcast with her. I made a commitment to serve others with my experiences. Good, bad, and ugly. I thought mostly bad and mostly ugly. The amazing part happened when I turned my mic on and my thoughts, feelings, and emotions flooded out of my mouth like a dam releasing for the first time.

Unshackling myself from the prison I had created felt like taking one-thousand-pound weights off my chest and shoulders. I felt like I could finally be seen, and I could finally stop lying to myself about the bad things I had gone through to try and be strong and I could just be. Now, don't get me wrong. Most of my initial vulnerabilities got cut out of the final edits because I may have finally been open to being open, but I was not ready to let everyone judge my openness. I let the thoughts flow, which was cathartic and its own special therapy. I thought I would be years in before I would be able to serve others with complete and total openness because I needed to build the strength it would take to accept other people's opinions of my experiences. Again, I was wrong. The uncomfortable path usually is the expedited path. Growth happens quicker than you could ever imagine when you're outside of your comfort zone.

I was thirty days into podcasting when I shared to the world I had spent most of my teen-adult years battling an eating disorder. I had barely even admitted this to two of the people closest to me before this. Even to my closest confidants, I danced around the subject, never fully being comfortable with discussing. To think I could morph from being so secretive to letting the world see every last inch of pain in this heart. The fear was gone. I didn't need strength to block opinions or judgments; in no time at all, that was the last thing on my mind. New strength came from each and every person who started sharing the impact I had made on their lives. Suddenly, being concerned with needing to have a wall of defense for the critics who would judge me were small fish in comparison to the impact I knew helping just one person feel like they weren't alone in wanting more out of life, or having a hard life, or a bad day, or feeling stuck, or not feeling anything at all. When I think of the compounding trickle effect of dismantling one toxic thought pattern in a person, it makes me cry every single time. And, to think, it all started with just allowing myself to be vulnerable. For that reason alone, I will forever be thankful for the medium of podcasting in allowing me to serve my community, be an authentic parent and partner, and show up for myself the way I finally deserve.

Whether you're starting a podcast to make money, increase brand awareness, buy yourself more time, or just enjoy the process of learning and the sound of your voice, podcasting is a true choose-your-own-adventure process. Every adventure starts with making connections. But you have to be brave enough to dig in and be willing to share. It takes courage. Tiffany was terrified. But she challenged herself, overcame her fears, and connected. That's freedom!

So let's dive into some of the possibilities.

Make Your Mission Statement and Find Your Focus

Your mission statement and your focus go hand in hand, giving you a clear picture of exactly who you are, who your audience is, and what you're trying to accomplish.

So, for example, let's say *The Bert Show* was a lifestyle blog for single women looking to better themselves, spiritually, physically, and mentally. That would be our mission statement. Let that be our guide at first. Your mission statement can change as you get more experience. But I think for beginning podcasters using a one- or two-sentence mission statement as your lighthouse is pretty important.

> "You either walk into your story and own your truth, or you live outside of your story, hustling for your worthiness."
> —Brené Brown

And in a lot of cases, I've heard people use their mission statement as the produced intro for their podcast, which I don't think is a bad idea either. It tells the listener immediately right off the bat who you are and what you are. But let's get back to the focus. This book, for instance, is a fun podcasting guide that focuses solely on the content and delivery of material during a podcast.

In *Forbes*, Sarah Rhea Werner shares her mission statements as she writes about creating podcasts with purpose. Her mission statement for her *Write Now* podcast is: "I will use my podcast to share truth, creativity and encouragement with listeners to nurture, heal and inspire them—and in doing so, help make the world a better and more empathetic place." She also has one for her fictional podcast: "I will use my audio drama to tell a fun, entertaining story that evokes beauty and universal truths and reminds listeners that no matter where or who they are, they're not alone."[6]

6   Sarah Rhea Werner, "How to Craft Your Podcast's Mission Statement," *Forbes*, July 13, 2017, https://www.forbes.com/sites/

Here are some other examples of effective mission statements from some of the most well-known institutions. While they aren't specific to podcasts, you can see how their choice of words tells followers exactly what to expect:

American Red Cross: "The American Red Cross prevents and alleviates human suffering in the face of emergencies by mobilizing the power of volunteers and the generosity of donors."[7]

NASA: "Lead an innovative and sustainable program of exploration with commercial and international partners to enable human expansion across the solar system and bring new knowledge and opportunities back to Earth. Support growth of the nation's economy in space and aeronautics, increase understanding of the universe and our place in it, work with industry to improve America's aerospace technologies and advance American leadership."[8]

Nike: "To bring inspiration and innovation to every athlete in the world. (If you have a body, you are an athlete.) Our mission is what drives us to do everything possible to expand human potential. We do that by creating groundbreaking sport innovations, by making our products more sustainably, by building a creative and diverse

sarahrheawerner/2017/07/13/how-to-craft-your-podcasts-mission-statement/.

7   American Red Cross, "Mission & Principles," Redcross.org, 2018, https://www.redcross.org/about-us/who-we-are/mission-and-values.html.

8   NASA, "Our Missions and Values," ed. Rachael Blodgett, NASA, August 5, 2021, https://www.nasa.gov/careers/our-mission-and-values.

global team and by making a positive impact in communities where we live and work."[9]

NPR: "The mission of NPR is to work in partnership with Member Stations to create a more informed public—one challenged and invigorated by a deeper understanding and appreciation of events, ideas and cultures."[10]

Everything in this book is written with a similar focus. There are very few chapters on equestrian riding saddles. Why? Because that topic doesn't have anything to do with "A fun podcasting guide that focuses solely on the content and delivery of material during a podcast."

When you crack the mic each week, who are you trying to connect with and what's the point of your podcast?

Your answers might be

- "I will make each and every element of the stock market easy to understand so my audience can make wise and educated investments."

- "Through my horrific experience getting divorced, I will share both legal and emotional advice to navigate through divorce with grace and understanding."

- "I will educate on how hand puppetry is the most effective way of educating about Pagan Witchcraft."

---

9   NIKE, "About Nike," Nike News, 2021, https://about.nike.com/.

10   NPR, "Our Mission and Vision," NPR.org, accessed March 15, 2022, https://www.npr.org/about-npr/178659563/our-mission-and-vision.

No matter what, you must ask yourself, does the content you're about to deliver fit into your focus? If not, kiss that content goodbye.

Your One Thing

By now, you probably already know your one thing, and it's probably beyond the examples I gave earlier of puppetry, the stock market, and divorce. Maybe you envision a podcast dedicated to the science of sleeping well, where you're hosting guests who have the art of sleeping down to a science. Perhaps it's poetry. Whatever your subject matter, it must be your *one thing* for your show. Listeners subscribe to learn about a particular topic, or to be entertained by a particular style. So, as a general rule, mixing needlepoint and nutrition won't cut it, and neither will inviting a nonfiction biographer who writes one-thousand-page bricks of knowledge onto your happy little haiku podcast.

If you want to spend more time on your purpose, which can guide the unique content of your podcast, I've borrowed this exercise from my friend Chris Tuff, author of *The Millennial Whisperer* and *Save Your Asks*:

> Create two columns. Write down everything that gives you energy in one and everything that drains your energy in the other. Let this list grow and know there's no bad answer here.
>
> Then answer these questions:

1. Where do you lose time? What activities do you do that when you're doing them you forget that time exists—you forget that you're hungry and entirely consumed with the task at hand?

2. Are you a builder or maintainer? Do you like building new things and excel in a world of innovation and change? Or do you enjoy predictability, order, and proven constructs?

3. If you could do one thing all day, every day what would it be? With the exception of coming home to sleep, what job would you do *all day* for 14 hours? This is your time to dream.

4. How do you want to be remembered? In 100 years, what is it you want the world to remember about your impact?

5. What does success look like for you? How do you currently measure success?
   Remember:

- Most purpose statements start with "To."
- Write in the present tense.
- Choose words that Reflect Positive Action.
- Keep it short.[11]

This chapter is about possibilities. Now's the chance to really think about the possible focus of your podcast,

---

11   Chris Tuff, *The Millennial Whisperer: The Practical, Profit-Focused Playbook for Working with and Motivating the World's Largest Generation* (New York: Morgan James Publishing, 2019).

because once you get started, you'll want to keep going, especially when you consider the other king out there in addition to content—cash.

Shake Your Moneymaker

I like money. There. I said it. I'm a fan of it. I know a lot of people say, "I'd do this job for free because I love it that much." Man, I sure do admire those liars. For me, the key is finding something you love doing that's rewarding. Radio has been so rewarding for me on a few levels that I won't bore you with, but I promise you one of those rewards has been a paycheck. And I don't think it's terrible to say, "I'd like to make some money off this podcast."

At *The Bert Show*, we increased our revenue by *eight times* as we went to nearly four million downloads per month. In less than a year, we were earning twenty times more than we ever had before! (Even as I wrote this book those numbers continued to grow; currently up to six million downloads per month.) How?

We learned to monetize our podcast, and man, did we learn some lessons. I'll get into some specifics about making money in a moment, but first, a few basics.

Your show has valuable content, not only to listeners but also to outside companies. This requires a mindset shift. Somebody's probably willing to pay you $250 to have their product mentioned on your show. So think of ways you can benefit from this. Let's say your podcast is about house cleaning, and you discuss a locally made, organic dishwashing detergent. Listeners want to buy the detergent—but where and how? That's where advertising and sponsorship come in. Just as companies will pay money to have their products stickered across the side of a bus or screaming from a billboard, they will pay you to help sell what they produce. Think of NASCAR with all those sponsors painted on the car. You're the car. How many of those sponsors do you want in your podcast? The more you have, the more money you make, but you *must* retain your credibility. Too many sponsors or ones that don't fit your brand make you susceptible to looking inauthentic.

I'll discuss more returns on your investment throughout this book, and in detail in chapter 5. (Actually, someone else will discuss the returns on your investment later in this book because while I do like making money, I hate talking numbers. But there are some who do, so I'll lean on them hard later in the book.) My focus is here: the biggest return on investment of a podcast is *connection*. Most podcasters started out because they needed an excuse for creating an experience and connection with people.

Take, for example, Tyler Jorgenson. Before he became the host of the *BizNinja Radio Show* on ABC News, he was just another eager person looking to expand his network and broaden his knowledge. There were people he wanted to connect with and learn from, but asking them to sit down for a phone call seemed like a bit of an "ask-hole" move—a term my friend Chris Tuff came up with for his book, *Save Your Asks*.

For Tyler, podcasting started so he could connect with like-minded professionals. He wanted both an excuse and a shortcut to learning new things while growing his network, like so many other aspiring podcasters. Now, people appear on *BizNinja Radio Show* out of a mutual desire to connect (they're also often leads for Tyler—can you say quid pro quo?).

And deep down, those same people want to be *heard*. You'll hear a lot about CPM and other listener-based measures, but if you're professional and your podcast sounds good, then you can get almost anyone to join you. A podcast is a gift.

> "The future is in curation, not creation. While Joe Rogan made more than $100 million with his Spotify podcast deal, Spotify's market value jumped a half billion after announcing the news. Eventually, the big money comes from people bringing shows together."—**Tom Schwab**, author of *Podcast Guest Profits: Grow Your Business with a Targeted Interview Strategy* and Founder/CEO of Interview Valet

Oh, You Really Want to Monetize It?

Did I mention I'm a fan of getting paid? This is next-level moneymaking stuff:

Nick Loper of Side Hustle Nation came up with this nifty list of cashing in on your expertise, which I've edited to provide some easy explanations.

Twelve Ways to Monetize a Podcast

1. Referral sponsorships: By mentioning a company's products, you can often get free products or services from them for yourself.

2. Traditional sponsorships: These generate money through the CPM. You can find sponsors through such sources as AdvertiseCast, Libsyn, True Native Media, Adopter Media, and Ad Results Media.

3. Sell your own products: Maybe you've written a book, or you have some hot new merchandise. What better way to advertise than through your podcast?

4. Sell your own services to listeners: This is the perfect opportunity to attract people to coaching, courses, or masterminds.

5. Sell your own services to guests: Build the kind of relationships where guests are willing to buy something from you after appearing on the show.

6. Sell your guests' products as an affiliate: And now the relationship is reciprocated.

7. Sell your guests' services as an affiliate: See above.

8. Listener donations: You can set up a pledge page on Patreon.com. If listeners like you enough, they may send Amazon gift cards or PayPal donations.

9. Repurpose your content: As Nick explains, his original *Side Hustle Path* series on Amazon was almost entirely derived from podcast content.

10. Syndicate your show to YouTube: Built-in advertising services allow you to earn even more money in passive income.

11. Charge your guests: This may not be your cup of tea, but if you have a loyal, dedicated audience, some guests may want to pay to reach those listeners for forty-five minutes so much that they consider it a wise investment of their advertising budget dollars.

12. Paywall old episodes: Charge a couple of bucks for past recordings, and it adds up.[12]

"The Riches Are in the Niches"

The first thing someone will ask you when you have a podcast is, "How many people do you have listening each week?" It's not always the right focus. It's the difference between having a podcast about role-playing games in general or, more specifically, a niche podcast specifically for Dungeons and Dragons or Final Fantasy.

CPM

CPM stands for cost per mille (thousand, in Latin) or the cost per thousand plays of each advertisement. Absorb this term. When we started our podcast, my business partner negotiated a two CPM for us. I didn't have any idea what

12 Nick Loper, "12 Ways to Monetize a Podcast - plus My Actual Results," Side Hustle Nation, November 21, 2020, https://www. sidehustlenation.com/monetize-a-podcast/.

that meant and wasn't even aware that's how we got paid on the podcast because, as I said before, I hate talking numbers. **Big mistake.** Only when we dissolved our partnership and I started doing the homework did I come to understand that the average CPM is about fifteen. To this day, I don't know what he negotiated for himself, but I do know that, because I allowed myself to be unaware, my show only got 2CPM of the advertising dollars coming in. I put this on me. You have to have a basic working knowledge of the money coming in and going out or people could take advantage of you. Again, this was on me, and I have nobody to blame but myself. When I figured it out, I made adjustments, changed podcast hosts, and immediately made seven times what we were making.

I also know one major podcasting host who had no idea how his network was getting paid on his show. Not a clue. Never even heard the term CPM. By the time he realized the network was giving him such a tiny percentage of the ad revenue, he and his team were already into a contract and out hundreds of thousands of dollars.

Meditate on This

So, sure, you're going to make some money from your show. But the beauty of podcasting lies in its ability to allow hosts to pursue passions that have been slowly smoldering while they work their day jobs. "I don't know why everybody thinks they have to do something forever," says

Chris Krimitsos, whose wife, Katie, is a prime example of making her little niche pay off in big ways.

As an early mover in the podcast industry, Katie was one of the first businesswomen to host *Biz Women Rock*, earning close to a six-figure income while working only thirty-five hours a week and raising a family. But after five years, with a second daughter on the way, Katie decided she was ready to sunset her role at *Biz Women Rock* and make a transition. "When we looked into the meditation niche, we found there was nothing specifically geared toward women," says Chris, who, with Katie, began listening to as many meditation podcasts as they could find. Many of them failed to state the intention of the meditation, which can leave listeners confused. Others were too complicated for people looking for a simpler way to get started, which made up a large percentage of her desired potential audience. So when they launched the Women's Meditation Network, they made sure to include intentions and create meditations that speak to millennials.

"As simple as it sounds, these were groundbreaking things for this space," says Chris. "And then because she takes it seriously, she's consistent. She's always launching." So the Women's Meditation Network then branched out and launched sleep meditations for women. From the sleep meditation, it took only three and a half months for her entire network to hit a million downloads, which is incredible. Katie was able to generate revenue by attracting a unique audience with her specific topics, gaining listeners who then referred her podcast to friends and family members. Her shows also immediately convey benefits to the audience, walking them through exactly what they'll get out of the show, whether it's a morning meditation or a guided relief from anxiety and stress.

Katie also practiced the mantra of "start ugly," calling her show *Women's Meditation Network*, which is the name of the business. But then she and Chris realized through search engine optimization (SEO) research that when searching for meditation information, the first thing people type is "meditation." So the show is now called *Meditation for Women*. Says Chris, "It was a very simple transition, but it worked."

Okay, you have a solid grasp of the possibilities of podcasting, right? Because it's time to move on to the people who are going to make these possibilities a reality: your audience.

NOW HEAR THIS

- Start ugly. Think about the "long game" when cutting your first podcast. It won't be good, and that's okay. Have patience. Most podcasts "podfade" because of impatience.
- Create a mission statement.
- Focus on one thing. *Your* thing. Not the thing you think people want to hear. Focus on what you want to say!
- Learn the right way to monetize your podcast.
- Get as specific as you can. The riches are in the niches in some cases.

CHAPTER 2:

Who Cares (Besides Your Mom)?

Tom Schwab knows more about successful podcasting than almost anybody else on the planet. In 2014, he realized that targeted podcast interviews tap into existing audiences, much like guest blogging. The result was Interview Valet, a company that connects podcasters with guests, driving millions upon millions of downloads for his clients. Tom is also the author of *Podcast Guest Profits: Grow Your Business with a Targeted Interview Strategy* and a genuinely good guy who was gracious enough to lend his expertise for this book—in this case, on the people who care: your audience.

"You're judged by the people who you associate with, the quality of the people you have on your show," says Tom. "And there are currently 1.8 million podcasts out there. Many of them are what I call 'Wayne's World' podcasts, two guys in their mom's basement."

If somebody hears you, says Tom, they Google you and they find you on that podcast. Chances are they'll make an instant decision on your quality, and "Wayne's World" is not going to cut it. "You want to make sure that whoever finds you, wherever they find you, that it helps your brand too." Tom adds how studies show the average podcast listener is above-average education, with above-average income. By definition, they're early adopters. But as of this writing, 57 percent of Americans over twelve years of age listen to podcasts—which means your audience is waiting for you.

You have your podcast. You have your vision. You know what you want to do.

But who is it you want to be talking to? Are you talking to one specific person, or a huge group of listeners?

Now that you've learned about all the possibilities, this chapter is all about your audience. We'll talk about building a cult following later in the book; for now, let's focus on the simple act of reaching listeners—the type of listeners who will remain loyal and help you generate genuine connection.

> "If you're going to suck at something, at least suck when there are fewer people listening. Some of the benefits of starting ugly are to work out those kinks as you grow your audience."—**Chris Krimitsos**

One Person—or One Million?

I don't necessarily talk to one person. I talk to one gender, because communicating to a twenty-one-year-old woman is so different from talking to a forty-nine-year-old woman. And my demographic really is women between the ages of twenty-one and forty-nine. So I've got people on my show who communicate with the younger demo. But for me, it's gender. You have to know who your audience is, and you have to stick to your one thing. I work with one podcaster who also has an audience of predominantly women. But every now and then he throws something in about topics that are not primarily targeted to women, such as UFC or boxing, which are generally liked by more men than women. I love sports more than anybody else, but I have to stick to what interests my audience.

Staying focused on your one thing attracts your audience and keeps that audience loyal. I see any additional listeners as icing on the cake.

What happens if you launch your show for middle-aged women, but all of a sudden it attracts a Gen Z audience?

My advice: stay authentic. If you try to cater to your audience, you're screwed. And it doesn't necessarily have to be a gender and age thing. If you are doing a podcast about therapy, stick to therapy topics, and don't talk about anything outside of therapy. People are coming to you for a specific reason. Maybe your niche is plumbing, or maybe your niche is accounting. Give them what they want and do not surprise them.

William Corbin of Sound That Brands brings up *The Message*, which is co-produced by GE and geared toward engineers. "I would have to imagine that any engineer listening to that podcast will favor GE and their buying decisions," he says, "just to ensure the podcast sticks around because nobody wants to lose it."

In 2006, 22 percent of Americans twelve years of age or older were familiar with podcasting.[13]

In 2021, 78 percent of Americans in this demographic—222 million—are now familiar with podcasting.

In 2006, 11 percent of Americans twelve years of age or older were listening to podcasts.

In 2021, 57 percent of Americans in this demographic—162 million—are now listening to podcasts.

Eighty million Americans twelve years of age or older now listen to podcasts weekly.

US weekly podcast listeners now average eight podcasts per week.

---

13   Edison Research and Triton Digital, "The Infinite Dial 2021," Edison Research, March 11, 2021, http://www.edisonresearch.com/wp-content/uploads/2021/03/The-Infinite-Dial-2021.pdf.

In radio, the theory is that you have eight seconds to grab someone's attention. Podcasting gives you a lot of grace here. Most people in a podcasting audience listen to 80 percent of an episode. Don't be fooled by this statistic. This might be true for regular listeners. But a new listener needs to be gripped quickly so you build loyalty which, in turn, is rewarded with longer listening. Nobody likes waiting for content, no matter what the medium. For me, when I listen to a podcast, you better get to it within the first thirty seconds. I don't want to fast forward. I have to get to the info that I'm looking for. There are some really popular podcasters who I've heard go up to fourteen minutes with nothing but ads or talking about their projects. And that absolutely drives me crazy. But I guarantee they would have never done that when they first started. You've got to get into your topic as quickly as possible. There are just way too many options now, way too many podcasts to be messing around with your audience because it's too easy to find something else. A good tease or a "table of contents" in the beginning of your podcast can be super helpful. But it has to be done correctly. More on that later.

Do Your Homework

How do you know whether or not your audience actually cares about your content? It's partly instinctual. And your numbers are going to show if your audience cares and is still listening. But you have to do your homework, just like before you even start your podcast. There's got to be a reason why you're starting that podcast. So knowing your audience and doing your homework on what you're going to be talking about should lead you down the right path. If your podcast is about relationships, find sources online that deliver similar material and put your unique spin on the topic. You are what separates you from everybody else. You can't be copied. You don't have to reinvent the wheel. If you find a podcast you love and it's in your interest zone, repurpose some of that material and make it your own. No, don't copy it. But if you find it interesting, chances are really good your audience will find it interesting too. Again, the difference is *you*. Your unique spin. Your unique connection to the content.

> "I've been podcasting for a while—before it was a thing. For me, there was always something to putting your thoughts together and expressing them in different forms to both entertain and educate people at the same time. It's an art, and in a way, it's helped me grow as a person. It's built a connection between myself and my listeners in a way that I feel responsible for an hour of their lives every week. My podcast may be small, but it means something, and I take it seriously. You get to crack a mic and enter someone's life for an hour—what do you want them to take away from spending that time with you? I think about that every week, and it's forced me to focus on my craft and myself in a way that I never have."—**Moe Mitchell**, host of *In The Moement* and co-host of *The Bert Show*.

R-E-S-P-E-C-T

We respect our audience, and we hear them. We treat them with respect, even if they have a totally different idea than we do. Some podcasters like to beat the crap out of their audience, but we're not like that at *The Bert Show*. We'd rather hear your side and then, if we need to, respectfully disagree with you.

We're people who have mics in front of us—we're no more special than a bus driver, a nurse, a teacher, a mom. In fact, we're *less* special, because we go in and riff on each other for hours. So, instead, our job is to make the audience feel special.

On that front, we can all take a lesson from Kristin Ingram, the host of *Small Biz Mama*. As a busy wife, mother, and entrepreneur who was (and still is) juggling the complexities of being a CPA all while serving her community, she began to lose sight of one of the most important pieces of the puzzle—taking care of herself. Many of her listeners have found themselves in the same boat, and they tune in and reach out to her because she doesn't wear any sort of chip on her shoulder. Instead, she goes above and beyond to wear her heart on her sleeve.

Kristen makes an effort to talk to those who reach out to her as her podcast guides others through the struggle. She makes a point to reply to emails, feature her listeners, and more. Overall, she goes above and beyond to ensure she helps others to feel less vulnerable, isolated, or overwhelmed. And that's exactly why Kristin has developed a concentrated but fervent following of listeners who see her as a good friend rather than a face. She makes a point to never hold back on any emotionality—and that's exactly the respect your listeners both want and deserve.

Your audience has a million opportunities to go elsewhere. So if they choose to sit with you for an hour of your podcast, you have to honor it. The most important thing in their life is their time, and they're investing their time in you—they're coming to you for a specific reason, either to escape or to learn something. You have got to take that seriously.

Once you have an air of arrogance, you lose your audience. So I've purposely built a staff of like-minded people who are humble and know that we're not better than anyone else. Our diversity is also key.

The Numbers Game

We've all heard about podcasters who are making millions off yoga practices for pregnant people and other super micro-focused content. There are only so many listeners out there who are expecting a baby and expecting to do sun salutations until the big day arrives. So they say the riches are in the niches, because when it comes to audience numbers, sometimes it's not necessarily just quantity. It's more about the quality of those listeners.

I've worked with a lot of podcasts that have a larger audience, but the smaller podcasts tend to have a lot more credibility, and more chances to make a lot of money. There might be a dentist who's making a ton of cash while getting only about eight hundred downloads per episode.

This happens a lot when people have influence with a really specific group and credibility. Even if they don't have a huge audience, they have huge opportunities. If you've got eight hundred people listening to each episode, are selling a high-end product or service that generates $1,000 in revenue for you, and even forty people are buying per month, you can make a boatload of money out of it.

Keep your focus on your niche instead of your numbers, and you'll attract more loyal listeners. When you first start a podcast and you've got a new audience, it's all about credibility, the way you communicate, and your connection. The only way to build that audience is for them to know you, love you, and trust you. And if you're not going headfirst in a credible way or an intimate way, your audience can find fifty other podcasters who are talking about the same stuff you are. The goal isn't to have them like you. The goal is to have them *love* you. So if you miss a week, they're actually upset. You're getting all sorts of complaints about it.

If They Complain, Refrain!

Dan Miller, the host of *48 Days to the Work You Love*, has received his fair share of complaints—but they're not the ordinary type of complaints. Rather than mean messages pouring through his inbox or pleas for different subject matter, his listeners often request for him to be sparing with bringing on guests. Why? They prefer his authenticity.

> He's grown a strong following as a man who knows what he's talking about, which is why his listeners want him and *only* him. Apparently, his guests just don't have the chops that he has. For that reason, he tends to only bring on a few guests a year and tries to make sure the topic isn't too stale.
>
> We'll be talking more about Dan's ability to incorporate the needs and wants of his listeners throughout the book. Take notes on this man's ability to retain his loyal listeners—if they complain, he listens.

The only way to find love from your listeners is through credibility, communication, and intimacy. This lasts until the very final moment of your podcast when you can tease what's coming up in the next one. So that means preparing in advance.

Many podcasters—especially new podcasters—have one show scheduled. When it ends, they have nothing for next week. This may work when you're a known podcast— Joe Rogan has his loyal audience and they don't care what he's going to talk about next week. They're tuning in no matter what. But if you're a new podcast, you want to give them a reason to come back next week with some kind of sensational tease. It becomes embedded in them: "On Tuesday, I've got to check that podcaster on yoga poses for pregnant women, not only because I love them but also because they're covering the material I read that intrigued me the week before." It might be a great idea to suggest setting an alarm on their phone so they don't miss your award-winning teased podcast.

Advertisers and Audiences

Let's flip the script for a moment. With great content, you're more likely to engage an audience that trusts you—and will trust your advertisers, too, which means more revenue. As Kurt Kaufer writes for *Forbes*: "Advertisers can rest assured that the vast majority of people that tune into a podcast will actually listen to ads, unlike the viewability challenges often associated with digital video. Various sources agree that podcast consumers listen to at least 80% of each episode."[14]

Kaufer cites a four-thousand-person survey that found 90 percent of audiences listen to podcasts at home. "This type of focused and personal listening can help to drive the efficiency associated with podcast advertising and generate leads," he writes. "Advertisers can take advantage of these engaged listeners by creating relationships with podcast hosts, onboarding them to their product or service, having them become enthusiastic brand advocates themselves and leveraging the power of their live endorsement in the context of the show." Incredibly, he adds, almost half of podcast consumers surveyed in one report "said they believe

---

14 Kurt Kaufer, "Who Listens to Podcasts (and How Can You Reach Them)?," *Forbes*, May 21, 2021, https://www.forbes.com/sites/forbesagencycouncil/2021/05/12/who-listens-to-podcasts-and-how-can-you-reach-them/.

that podcast hosts they regularly listen to actually use the products/services mentioned on their podcasts."

It's a win-win-win when you engage your audience effectively. You get a loyal following, advertisers get to connect, and your listeners get quality content and recommendations for products and services that match their lifestyle.

Social Media

Social media can be a really helpful tool when it comes to promoting your content, but most podcasters do it incorrectly. Teasing your content properly is everything. In other words, you have to make your tease super intriguing to force someone to change their routine and check out your podcast. For example, you might tease, "Episode 22 of *Two Men Talking About Nothing Important*: chatting with #ChrisPratt." That kind of tease might get the attention of Chris Pratt fans. But you're going for a wider audience. Your tease has to make the ambivalent Chris Pratt fan interested. Tease them with a highlight from the interview:

- "#ChrisPratt tells us how he knew his marriage was over on the *Two Men Talking About Nothing Important* podcast"
- "#ChrisPratt hates #ChrisPine for good reason!"
- "Chris Pratt tells us why he's insecure about his private parts on the latest *Two Men Talking About Nothing Important podcast*"

The difference is massive. Sensationalize your teases, link to your podcasts, and intrigue a potential listener with social media.

"One of the things that I tell people when it comes to social media is if you wait too long, then you're going to make mistakes," says Chris Krimitsos. "You're building a social media presence, but you haven't launched a podcast yet. Your business is growing, your speaking places, whatever. But you haven't launched your podcasts yet. By definition, you're not going to be as good on episode one as you're going to be on episode one hundred." Here we go again: *start ugly*.

And trust me, ugly is the operative word for the next chapter, as I share how to handle the toughest stuff in the podcasting business.

🎧 NOW HEAR THIS

- A new podcasting audience is fickle. You have to capture their attention quickly if you're going to build loyalty.
- You are judged by the quality of people on your show.
- Be aware and *smart* with your social media presence. Think of social media as a commercial for a product.
- The riches are in the niches. In other words, don't get caught up in massive numbers.

CHAPTER 3:

The Uncomfortable Parts

If I were to tell you right now that you would have to set up an interview every single day for the next one hundred days, could you do it? Or would you get burned out on your subject matter? Now, record a short voice memo even on your phone of you pretending to podcast. Play it back. Listen to the sound of your voice. How does your voice sound to you? Do you hate your voice?

Those questions are at the core of what this chapter is about: the uncomfortable parts of podcasting, from big-picture planning and addressing pain points to hearing yourself and asking yourself the right questions.

"The hardest thing about podcasting is being consistent," says Moe Mitchell, my *Bert Show* co-host. "Finding ways to create high-quality content worth listening to week in and week out? It isn't as easy of a task as people believe it to be. Anyone can talk for an hour, but few people can be entertaining for an hour. One of the easiest ways to be constant is to be authentic—if you lean on that, focus on your strengths, and grow with your listeners, I think you can create something truly special."

That's the process that has helped Aryeh Sheinbein turn his podcast, *Inside the Lion's Den*, into an intellectual powerhouse (namely for financial minds). He calls it (no surprise) the "Lion's Den Concept."

Instead of looking for subject matter belonging to a saturated market where experts offer insight from every angle (and bore listeners with it), Aryeh makes a point to extract stories from guests who can shed light on unexplored places.

As Aryeh has learned, people *dig* the unknown—whether they're finance whizzes or fly-fishing connoisseurs. It's fun to learn about stuff, after all, and the internet is a big place—people can find information anywhere. If you can get people to do a double take because what you're going to talk about is interesting, bizarre, or outside the box, you're setting your podcast up for success.

I want that to really be absorbed. Talking versus being entertaining are two very different things.

Big-Picture Planning

Big-picture planning is critical for a new show or when you're doing a checkup to see if your show sucks. It's not nearly as much fun as just diving into an interview with

Julia Roberts, but it's the only way you're going to ever have a hope of landing an interview with Julia Roberts in the first place.

The big picture starts with the mission statement and the focus we discussed in chapter 1. Why am I listening to your podcast instead of somebody else's? Remember your one thing: Is it women's lifestyle? Is it entrepreneurship? Is it how to save money? Is it psychology?

If you've already started your show and are, say, eight episodes in, the content should be marrying up with the mission statement. That's what your audience is expecting. If you're starting to veer off into little offramps of your mission statement, that's okay. It just can't be a completely different highway.

Are You a Vitamin or a Painkiller?

My friends in the entrepreneurial world like to talk about the difference between a vitamin and a painkiller when it comes to launching products. A vitamin is "nice to have," while a painkiller is "need to have." We feel like we *should* use a vitamin, but we *want* to use a painkiller. (There's also candy, which gives us a temporary rush, but doesn't get us anywhere.) Your podcast can be all three—maybe a little sugar high at the beginning and useful for the long term. But ultimately, you want to produce a painkiller, helping your audience progress. That means either removing something that was troubling them or giving them something to help them move forward. A podcast-loving colleague of mine, for example, was considering getting an infrared sauna. When he went online to search for more information, he could not find any podcaster mentioning anything about infrared saunas. This is a case where creating a painkiller—a show on wellness devices, perhaps—is going to give a specific audience-specific knowledge and build loyalty, brand awareness, and sponsorship and revenue opportunities. We always strive to make *The Bert Show* a painkiller. We want them to *need* us to tweak their mood.

Stop Copying Me!

Joe Rogan is a really specialized talent. He's built up such credibility that I know I'm going to be a smarter person on a particular subject after listening to him. As of this writing, he's recorded nearly one thousand eight hundred episodes in eleven years, attracting more than 830 guests and notching more than two hundred million YouTube views of his top ten shows.

But you can't try to be the next Joe Rogan because he is an anomaly. So stop comparing yourself to him. The beauty of being Joe Rogan, the beauty of being Howard Stern, the beauty of being LeBron James or Jay-Z—anybody who is one of the greatest of all time in their respective fields—the G.O.A.T.s of the world, so to speak—is that they cannot be copied. You could try to do exactly the same stuff that any of these top-echelon people are going to do. You're never going to pull it off because the beauty of who they are is their uniqueness. So you have to create your own uniqueness.

> "The hardest thing about podcasting is being consistent. Finding ways to create high-quality content worth listening to week in and week out? It isn't as easy of a task as people believe it to be. Anyone can talk for an hour, but few people can be entertaining for an hour. One of the easiest ways to be constant is to be authentic—if you lean on that, focus on your strengths, and grow with your listeners, I think you can create something truly special."—**Moe Mitchell**

Adjusting Your Expectations

Going from radio to podcasting made me change my expectations big-time. In fact, just learning radio in the first place taught me some hard lessons about expectations. I've worked with some truly gifted entertainers in radio. I'm not one of them. I had to bust my butt from day one to figure out how to do it. So what sounds natural now was absolutely not natural in the beginning. I had to work on it every single day. Now I'm pretty comfortable. But I'm no different from a beginning podcaster. I was stumbling. I didn't know what to do. I didn't know how to edit. I didn't know what to talk about. I had no focus. I was cracking the mic and I was talking as quickly as I could just to get the segment over because I was so nervous. Eventually, I developed the skills. You can teach yourself how to be a great talent, as long as you adjust your expectations. Talent takes years to develop.

Just ask Tyler Jorgenson. Remember him? We talked about his reasons for starting the *BizNinja Radio Show*. While he was motivated to connect with like-minded professionals and grow his knowledge, he couldn't get there overnight. Having conversations with the people he wanted to learn from—despite his go-getter attitude—could only take him so far. Why? You guessed it: his expectations were too high.

Tyler thought it'd be easy enough when he started out on local stations. But without much behind-the-scenes assistance, he found himself barely keeping his head above water. Tyler had to put in a lot of elbow grease between lining up interviews, making sure his guests actually showed up to them, and so on. Without a producer or team, the struggle was real.

As you can imagine, Tyler's early days in podcasting were riddled with complete overwhelm. Eventually, of course, he learned the ropes and gained momentum to get to where he is now. But it took a lot of trial, error, and plenty of frustration before he was able to find his feet and start shooting for the stars.

So avoid falling into the trap so many podcasters fall into by expecting too much, too soon. Many podcasters never get past that first stage of learning—which is exactly where the opportunity to make a long-lasting impact lies. Patience, patience, and more patience. Give yourself a lot of grace. This is new to you. You're learning. Be patient while growing an audience. Even with the help of my twenty-seven-market radio network in which we promote our Pionaire Podcasting network shows, it's a slow build. A painstakingly slow build.

Ten Truths about Podcasting

1. You have about a minute to engage an audience.
2. One sentence defines every piece of content.
3. Connecting with your audience is different from talking to an audience.
4. Choose the right players for your podcasting team.
5. Motivate your audience to never tune out.
6. Work smartly on well-focused show prep.
7. An audience can't love you if they don't know you.
8. Content and audience have to match.
9. Good show schedules boost confidence.
10. Every podcast must end with four elements: gratitude for listening, a suggestion to subscribe, a plug for next week's episode, and details about when it will be posted.

Remember, we're not trying to build an average podcast. We're trying to build an exceptional one. The way to do that is to connect. And you just can't be a fact speaker, rambling on about the statistics behind optimal hydration or the meaning of Led Zeppelin song lyrics. You have to connect with the material and love it. Emotional details are way more important than physical details. Linking emotions and facts is paramount to engaging your audience. Let me repeat that. How you *feel* is more important than the event. How you felt while shopping for wedding rings is way more important to an audience than the physical details of you looking at wedding rings.

The Sound of Your Voice

It's a scientific fact that many of us hate the sound of our own voice, thanks to the way we process acoustic information through the vibration of tiny little bones called ossicles. I've been doing radio ads from Atlanta for twenty years, and I can't listen to our best stuff. When my voice comes on the radio in a commercial, I still turn that thing off. I absolutely hate it and I've never gotten used to it, ever. When I first got into radio, there were these big booming voices, deep fake voices. And I came in with my squeaky voice, my high-pitched voice.

Look at Ryan Seacrest, who was once working on an alternative station in Atlanta as a part-timer and, from what I understand, lost his show because the program director hated his squeaky voice. So he actually got fired from his first radio gig because of the sound of his voice. And still, Ryan Seacrest became *Ryan Seacrest*. He laughs at this story now because it was so shortsighted.

The point is: get over it because nobody cares about the sound of your voice unless it's really freaking annoying. Nobody cares about it. What they care about is what's coming out of your mouth. You're going to be twenty times more critical of your own voice than anybody else will be. The last thing in the world anybody should be concerned with is the sound of their voice. It is what you're saying that matters. Having a different voice is an advantage. Not a disadvantage.

Rehearsing and Listening with a Critical Ear

You know all those podcasters making a bazillion dollars? Go back and listen to their first podcast. It's so painful. Nobody's podcast is going to be really good the first time. Nobody's. Period. Or the second one. Or the third one. It's like anything else; you try to make little improvements each and every week. And you rehearse.

The first podcast you record? Don't put it online. It is such an odd feeling to be in front of a microphone for the very first time and, as I mentioned, listen to your voice in your headphones. So while you're trying to do that and work through your material, your podcast is not going to be good. Why would you introduce yourself to an audience when the quality of your podcasts is bad? Yes, you should start ugly, but if you can, you should spend weeks, if not months, rehearsing before you launch your podcast.

I've known guys in the sports industry who used to sit up in the stands at sporting events with just a recorder when they knew they wanted to be a sportscaster, and they would call the sports game just to themselves from the cheap seats. They did that for months and months and months before they put together any kind of air check and pitched a radio station or a TV station for a gig. So rehearse. It may be uncomfortable, but remember, the thing about podcasting is that anybody can do it, which is great, but anybody can do it, which is also really bad.

It's also uncomfortable to listen with a critical ear because you don't know what's good and you don't know what's bad initially, and you won't know that until you start to get slightly more comfortable on a mic. And that takes months. So do what you're going to do those first couple of months. Don't put it online; rehearse. And then when you have a little bit more of a comfort level, put it on and edit the snot out of it.

A lot of podcasters, especially new podcasters, feel like the podcast has to be an hour. But if you're brand new to podcasting, you can't plan on being entertaining for sixty minutes. And when you start those rehearsal sessions, I would start them really, really small. Give yourself five minutes, then give yourself seven minutes and then give yourself nine minutes because your research takes way longer than you think it's going to. Even when you're podcasting, by the time you're done, if you got twenty-five minutes of material, I bet five of it is really good. But your five will go to seven, will go to nine, will go to eleven, and at some point or another, you'll get up to an hour.

Dealing with the Critics

Yes, you will have critics, no matter how perfect your podcast is. Sometimes the critic is you. When you have that little critic in your head while you're delivering your podcast, you'll never be great. You have to be unapologetically you. I am super competitive.

And if it's an outside critic, someone who posts a negative comment on social media or otherwise spews a little venom into your podcasting life? I know there is nothing more a hater wants than to get into my head. I won't allow it. They don't get to win. And you shouldn't allow someone else's judgment to keep you from being your best.

Take it from Tim Ferris, who offers these eight tactics for dealing with haters in *Tools of Titans*:[15]

1. It doesn't matter how many people don't get it. What matters is how many people do.
2. 10% of people will find a way to take anything personally. Expect it and treat it as math.
3. When in doubt, starve it of oxygen.
4. If you respond, don't *over*-apologize.
5. You can't reason someone out of something they didn't reason themselves into.
6. "Trying to get everyone to like you is a sign of mediocrity. You'll avoid the tough decisions, and you'll avoid confronting the people who need to be confronted." —Colin Powell
7. "If you want to improve, be content to be thought foolish and stupid."—Epictetus
8. "Living well is the best revenge." —George Herbert

You're doing a podcast! The spineless critic doesn't have the guts to do what you're doing. Remember that.

The difference between being good and being great is being brave. Period. It's time to move on to being a partner with the other people behind your podcast.

---

15   Tim Ferriss, *Tools of Titans: The Tactics, Routines, and Habits of Billionaires, Icons, and World-Class Performers* (Boston: Houghton Mifflin Harcourt, 2016).

🎧 NOW HEAR THIS

- It's essential to do big-picture planning and have several shows in the pipeline.
- Practice authenticity—copying others is lame.
- Emotional details connect with listeners more than physical details.
- Get over the sound of your voice.
- Practice, practice, and practice again.

Part 2:

Your People

CHAPTER 4:

People on the Mic

My co-host, Moe Mitchell, has his own podcast, *In The Moement*, which is funny, insightful, and lifestyle-driven. It also speaks volumes to the importance of the people we put on the mic. Do you want to host a show solo, or include other like-minded, knowledgeable folks? How do you find quality co-hosts, and how do you make sure they're on brand with your consistent content designed to make an impact? I'll answer these questions, and more, in this chapter and the following, which are dedicated to the people who help make your podcast a success.

But first, I'll let Moe tell his own story of going solo:

I went to solo podcasting initially as a challenge to myself.

When I first began to podcast, I did it alone, but over time I just got comfortable with having a team. It was easier and I felt as if I needed it. After a while, quite a few people kept recommending that I give solo a shot and I did.

It was rough waters at first, feeling as if I needed to find a way to fill the same amount of time with the same level of entertainment without the benefit of being able to converse with and bounce off of other people.

After a couple of episodes, I feel like I found my groove and to my surprise it was a lot more natural than I anticipated; it was actually easier. It was easier to collect my thoughts and express them fully and more precisely. I feel like I found my comedic groove; I was able to mimic the things I do on stage more accurately and authentically behind a mic.

I'm a visionary and a thinker, and it made it a little simpler to capture my visions and put them into words when I was no longer focused on making someone else comfortable. It gave me the space that I needed to be more authentic in what I talk about and how I talk about it, which in turn has made it a more authentic "moment" with me.

It's become somewhat of a therapeutic moment with myself. That's priceless. I wasn't sure if it made my podcast better at first, but if I'm going with the feedback from listeners, it's miles better.

Doing a solo podcast is challenging. You have to find a way to be intriguing enough that people will actually want to sit through listening to you have a conversation with yourself. It might be a bit difficult for some people to think of themselves as that entertaining. It's not impossible though. I think it just requires a little more preparation. You have to have a clear vision on what you want the focus of your podcast to be: humor, informative, educational, etc.

Approach every week as a brand new one and give people reasons to look forward to you having something to say. Find something you have that people want and continue to pour into that every week, while leaning on whatever it is that you consider your strength.

Solo or Co-Host?

It's a simple equation, as far as I'm concerned. More people on the mic equals more headaches (No offense, *The Bert Show* team.). For me, having a co-host is a pain because I'd rather spend my time recording episodes on my own than comparing calendars to record together (Fortunately, we don't have this issue with *The Bert Show*. That said, additional hosts mean more people promoting the show into their orbits. And I've never done a solo show. I'm not talented enough to talk to myself for an hour. Plus, I love having others on my team score as much as I like scoring. I love setting people up and working as a team. The last maturation of my radio show was pretty seamless.

But it took me my whole career to figure out what makes a great team.

On the other hand, if you want to listen to a podcaster who is talented enough to pull off a consistently funny, relatable, authentic weekly show, check out Heather McMahan's *Absolutely Not*. So talented. So funny. And she is a great example of someone who knows how to deliver "A" material every week for an entire hour. Not many can do this. She needs nobody on this show with her. In fact, when she does have guests, I get kinda bummed out 'cause it takes away from listening to just Heather talk. Way more talented than I am. I could never do this!

However, if you're thinking about putting an ensemble cast together for your show, you can definitely make it work. Here are some things to consider to help you make the right decision for you.

Co-Host Cohabitation

The first thing to ask yourself when putting together this team is, "Are we going to be able to communicate with each other?" If you're reading this, the chances are good that you're a new podcaster. You're inexperienced. Your other hosts may be inexperienced. You all are going to have to make adjustments along the way and be able to communicate with honesty and without ego. This is *not* easy. The hosts might have different ideas on how to execute content.

It's incredibly important that you and your team are mature enough and have the empathy that will allow you to genuinely listen to each other and not be offended. The best way to ensure this: Hire someone who knows podcasting to act as a middleman—he or she can listen to all parties and make suggestions equally. (Heck, hire me so you and your hosts don't end up with a murder case on your hands.)

Managing yourself is a challenge, and I know few teams that do it well, without resentment or tension. If you don't manage it, you end up failing. Period.

The Cautionary Tale of *Call Her Daddy*

Call Her Daddy is a great example of a podcast imploding because of bad communication between co-hosts. In 2018, Alexandra Cooper and Sofia Franklyn launched the comedy podcast, discussing their exploits with men in New York City, soon building a cult following. When they shifted to a Barstool Sports platform, *Call Her Daddy* went from twelve thousand downloads to two million. But as they renegotiated their Barstool contract, Sofia said Alexandra stabbed her in the back, and the show went belly-up until Alexandra started it up again as a solo host—without the same chemistry from Sofia. See how pettiness, poor communication, and conflicting agenda can ruin a perfectly profitable good thing?

Values and Intentions

Surround yourself with people you trust, with no hidden agendas, who think of the product before themselves and have a positive attitude even when you guys are struggling. Want instant karma? *Good luck with that!* It took me an entire career to finally identify the right mix of people who genuinely cared about each other as people and cared as much about the product as I did. I had one staff member, behind my back, walk into our bosses' office and tell them either he or I had to go. Keep in mind the show was in my name. So it's a little like Questlove going to NBC and saying, "Look, either Jimmy Fallon has to go or me!"

I also interviewed one woman for a co-hosting position, ending with a tour of the station before I headed back to my office. I later heard that when I left her in the studio with some other personnel, she started telling them what the studio would look like when she was hired and how she'd rearrange the on-air staff seating when she took the job. Nope. She didn't land the job, and I ended up hiring the most loyal, authentic, funny co-host who made me a better person and professional.

The point? Hire people who share your values and sniff out bad intentions. Find the right fit for your personality and for your schedule. My personality radar is pretty good. But sometimes I didn't listen to it because I was too insecure to make the right personnel decisions. I didn't believe in my talent. Don't make that mistake. Believe in yourself!

You want to hear a great podcast that you can lose yourself in? Listen to *SmartLess*. Sean Hayes, Will Arnett, and Jason Bateman get it! I was skeptical at first because a lot of celebrity podcasters think, *If I just talk about my life, people will love it.* Um, *no*. Just because you're you, it doesn't make you entertaining. Also, putting a few A-listers on a podcast together could be a very cautionary tale because of egos. But these guys table their egos, are relatable, tell great stories, and have amazing chemistry. It's so fun to listen to. They must be making a boatload of money!

Define Roles

This is critical. Playing it by ear doesn't work! Let's underscore and bold and italicize and post this in big ol' neon letters: *Playing it by ear doesn't work.* I've seen so many shows implode because one person thinks they are doing more work than the other when the truth is they are working equally just on different things, but one puts more value on their aspect of the podcast. One host might be focusing on the content and show schedule. The other might be marketing and editing. Both are working. Just working differently. These roles will become increasingly clear as you start working together. Don't fight it. Go with each member's strengths.

Ryan Dobson, the co-host of *Rebel Parenting with Ryan & Laura Dobson*, teams up with his wife to help fellow parents navigate the hectic life of parenting. Together, they've learned the art of collaborating. And they're not just collaborating with one another: Ryan and Laura have an entire behind-the-scenes team they can always trust to get the job done right.

To Ryan, one of the most valuable life lessons is that success doesn't come from working on your weaknesses. Instead, Ryan believes the key lies in shifting your focus toward building on what you're already great at.

In other words, there's no use in trying to improve in something you're consistently weak in. Ryan finds a much better use of his time in tripling down on what he's great at. And he applies this same logic to his podcast. That's why he employs an A-team he can count on to crown his show with the "shine" it needs to impress listeners.

As somebody whose father was a radio "Hall-of-Famer," Ryan takes great pride (and emphasis) in his belief that "high-quality content is KING." The fact that Ryan can wholeheartedly trust his editors and engineers to get the job done right evokes a sense of freedom in him that he has fallen in love with, and I don't blame him. If you want that same feeling, then you ought to take notes from this man—and you also better ask yourself the hard questions.

For example, is one of you better at the transitioning in and out of topics? Is one of you a better reactor? How are you going to divide up the content? How are you going to filter the content before you start the podcast?

This is super important stuff. Ego will *kill* any relationship. Here comes the neon sign again! *Ego will kill any relationship.* It doesn't matter if it's marriage or dating or at work or with your parents. Ego kills *any* relationship, and business is no different. And when you're entertaining, you're already dealing with a certain amount of ego, right? And ego does *not* have to be a bad word. It's necessary. But you feel like you have something to say. You want to be heard. Your content is uber personal. You're invested in your own content. It's *really* hard to sacrifice your content for somebody else's. It's *so* hard. But you have to. You have to work as a team. You're in a relationship if your podcast has more than just you behind a mic.

If you can find someone to produce the show, someone you respect and you have the money, I would suggest finding someone who manages the other aspects.

For instance, one person might be doing the podcast schedule, booking guests, and marketing. The other person is editing, working on content, helping plan new shows, and more. These are the people behind the scenes—which is just what we'll discuss in the next chapter.

NOW HEAR THIS

- A solo podcast can be challenging. Consider a co-host—but most of all, go with what makes you comfortable.
- Roles will develop. Identify and amplify each other's talents.
- Make sure you and your team members can listen with empathy before deciding to work together. Ego will kill your podcast—and every relationship you're in.
- Surround yourself with people you trust.
- Define roles clearly and carefully.

CHAPTER 5:

People Behind the Scenes

The first guy I ever worked with in radio was Jack Diamond, a big-time radio personality. (His real name is Harvey Fischer.) I followed him from San Diego to Washington, DC, and for the first three-quarters of my career, I followed his lead, and his lead was a very structured show. There wasn't a lot of spontaneity to it. Jack would come in with all of the things that he was going to talk about—he had them all set and ready to go. He was reading jokes and stuff out of the pages of prep services; it was just super structured.

This was my approach for most of my career. But when I realized I wanted to do my own show, I knew I had to find a different mentor who did something totally different. And that's when I was hired by Kidd Kraddick, who

I felt more in line with as far as a radio personality. He would come in with one idea, and he was just so incredibly creative that he could structure an entire show around that one idea. At least that's what it looked like by the time he got in the studio. I don't know what he was doing behind the scenes, but I remember sitting at the radio station and watching him pulling out the *Dallas Morning News* and, in pencil, writing two or three things to talk about. The entire show was those three ideas that he had right before we went on air. So it was just a completely different experience than I had had with Jack Diamond.

For my own show, I started taking different elements from both of these guys. It was probably one-fourth Jack Diamond and three-fourths Kidd Kraddick. My story illustrates how important it is to have experiences and surround yourself with people who have very different ideas than you do, and then having the humility to listen to them take your ego out of it and execute an idea that you're not necessarily comfortable with.

I mentioned Aryeh Sheinbein and his "Lion's Den Concept"—the idea that people tune in to learn about the unknown because what's unknown is interesting. So he tries to feature guests who can shed light on the roads less traveled.

Aryeh knows—as I've learned—you can't plot some easy course that the other guys are already exploring. You need to be open-minded to thought that exists outside the box. Then you'll create an adventure where listeners will want to tag along.

The same goes when you're managing any business or company. If you don't listen to your advisers around you, and you think you're the smartest one in the room, you will not succeed long term.

With these two mentors, I was the person behind the scenes for many years, so I learned both sides, and sometimes the hard way. So I've devoted this chapter to all the people who help pull our show together, and how you can build a team in a much easier way.

Know Your Strengths and Weaknesses

When I was putting *The Bert Show* together, I knew I needed some balance. The entire show, for as long as we've been on, has been based on trying to get a room filled with people bringing different experiences to the table. When I first started, I had no hosting experience at all—I had just been a sidekick or a co-host on other people's shows. I knew I needed to hire support people who had a lot of experience with morning radio because, frankly, I didn't know what the heck I was doing. I was filling that experience gap with producers who had worked on morning shows and really knew what they were doing.

There's a tendency among new podcasters to bootstrap, roll up their sleeves, and do everything themselves. But if you're building something aspirational that has a strong foundation and can be monetized based on episodes and downloads, then trust other people to make you better and faster. You'll be able to produce more content. If you free yourself from the technicalities of doing all the junk behind the scenes, you can double your episodes. It's an investment in yourself and your future.

Know what you're strong at and know your weaknesses—where you need help. Then, hire the best and the people you trust to take over.

I know content. But what do I know about what mic to use or what do I know about marketing? Nothing. So I surround myself with the best people who will fill in those gaps. This also makes me a better talent because I don't have to worry about that stuff. I'm outsourcing to the experts. For me, the most important parts of a podcast are the delivery, homework, and content. By surrounding yourself with experts, you allow yourself to grow.

Managing the people involved in your podcast is one of the most difficult aspects of podcasting. So if you have the money to hire a consultant—someone who is hearing all the sides and is playing ambassador among everybody on the show—this is, far and away, the most advantageous route to take. It can be challenging to find a highly qualified consultant, but I know one.

(I'll endorse my own company here 'cause, hey, it's my book, and I can. At Pionaire Podcasting, we do all this for our shows. It's a talent owned and operated company. We're not suits. Our background is in being creative. No pressure, but you'll totally fail if you don't hire us, and, again, you'll be lonely the rest of your life because you failed miserably. Pionairepodcasting.com.)

The 30x Rule: How Great Managers Multiply Performance

In *Procrastinate on Purpose*, Rory Vaden makes an excellent case for delegating and outsourcing. "An inherent measure of our effectiveness as managers is our ability to create results through other people," he writes, adding that many managers have high standards that handicap our ability to delegate. "What we have noticed is that delegating is not a logical issue; it's an emotional one. We all know there are things we are doing that someone else could be trained to do, but we don't do it. Why not? One reason we often cite is just not having enough time to train other people to do it correctly. Unfortunately, those managers are making that decision rooted in an old paradigm of time-management thinking that is governed more by the urgency of today than the significance of tomorrow."[16]

As Vaden explains, the world's most effective managers (which he calls "Multipliers") have learned to adopt "significance" thinking as evidenced by "the 30x rule."

"The 30x rule says you should spend 30x the amount of time training someone to do a task than it would take you to do the task yourself one time," he writes. "Multipliers know that any task that takes you 5 minutes per day * 250 working days in a year = 1250 total minutes that will be

---

16 Rory Vaden, *Procrastinate on Purpose: 5 Permissions to Multiply Your Time* (New York: Perigee, 2015).

> spent on that task over the course of a year. So investing 150 minutes (30 X 5) in training someone to do a task that takes 5 minutes a day is still a very effective use of time. The reason is because if you divide 150 (time you spent training) into 1100 (the net amount of time it saves you over the course of a year after you deduct the time you spent training), then that yields what we refer to as a 733% ROTI—Return On Time Invested."
>
> Once you understand the 30x rule and the significance calculation, Vaden explains, you realize the real truth to why we don't delegate. We think, "Someone else won't be able to do it as well as I can." But you multiply your time by giving yourself the emotional permission to invest time into things today that create more time tomorrow.

Outsourcing 101

What brings a podcast to life best is when people finally decide to stop trying to edit it themselves and outsource it for $100 or an affordable going rate. This frees up your time and allows you to focus on research and other important elements of your show. But first you can find confidence in outsourcing by looking at your numbers; later, you can add other elements to outsource and delegate to your people behind the scenes.

Step one: Start keeping track of your metrics. How much do you make per episode? If you can outsource for less money than you make per episode and outsourcing allows you to produce additional episodes, then you're able to outsource sooner than you think. You'll have better use of your time and will make more money by creating additional episodes: maybe two per week instead of just one. It's not just outsourcing for the sake of outsourcing. You're outsourcing to create new dollars because you can make more money by going deeper and building your brand there. So really monitor your numbers, value their time, and see what you believe your time's worth.

Step two: Find someone else to edit your podcast. You don't have to hire the best; if you can outsource for $50 an episode just to take the tasks off your hands, even if it's not the ideal person, you'll get a head start on finding more time and money. I cannot stress how important this is. If you're a new podcaster, outsourcing is absolutely mandatory. (And if you're experienced, it's strongly encouraged.)

I know it's hard to give up control of the editing when only *you* truly know how you want your podcast to sound. Our egos are so tied up in our product that we might not really be giving our audiences only the "A" material and leaving the rest on the cutting room floor. Bottom line: outsourcing is too important a job to take lightly. It opens you up to do more promotion, connect with more people, produce more episodes, and get more people listening to your podcast. Outsourcing is an investment, and it allows you to make a bigger impact.

Step three: Outsource the moneymaking part of your podcast. Sites such as Patreon connect you to listeners who are willing to pay money for more episodes. If you have fifty people paying you $5 a month for an extra episode, that's $250 bucks a month, which allows you to hire podcast editors.

From the Editor's Eye

To give you a glimpse of why outsourcing the editing is a no-brainer, we picked the brains behind *The Bert Show*, Josh Hall, who makes us sound about a trillion times better with his tricks of the trade.

How frequently do you get content to edit?

I edit for different folks as frequently as they need. With podcasting, typically that's a weekly cycle. In a perfect world, you'd get a few days to work on an edit, but oftentimes schedules require fast turnaround. It's helpful to allow a day as well for all the participants to be able to listen back to the audio and make sure it's up to spec before uploading for distribution.

How do you decide what stays and goes?

Often you'll get notes from the recording session about important areas to address with minute and second marks. These will typically be of the "so and so forgot something and we had to look it up; edit at 32 mins and 15 secs" variety—maybe notated as 32m 15s, or the most common 32:15. Again, sometimes in a quick turnaround situation, one needs to get right to work.

I suppose there are two types of edits—what you might call logical and emotional edits. Logical edits are stutters or word fumbles that are common in everyday speech, including long pauses, coughs, sniffles, phone rings, someone banging into the mic stand, or even the occasional belch.

Emotional edits are based on what's said contextually. For example, if I tell a story where I pause or stumble, it might reveal something I don't say directly. Does my pause carry the same emotional resonance if edited shorter? Does the impact increase or decrease with an edit? That sort of thing.

A middle space between logical and emotional might be the time it takes to breathe. If you've ever heard an edit of a solo voice speaking with no time to breathe, you can imagine the nonstop energy of going and going without taking even a second to reflect or inhale as the most basic function of being in a body could be exhausting to the ear as it doesn't reflect a reality that anyone experiences in talking with another person. Or at least not the kind you'd want to listen to again!

A good edit might ebb and flow—always with remembering the final listener experience. Will they be bored or interested? Is the extra detail in the story distracting or does it enhance the understanding and impact of the payoff for sitting through it?

How do you work on the transitions?

Besides editing audio, I might be asked to help with additional sounds blended together with music and sound to help create a mood for the final production or even a theme (or bed) to talk over for a specific podcast.

Typically, these would be produced in pre-production, so I'd have them ready when it's time to edit and mix the final podcast. I could reuse them each week.

What tips can you share with new podcasters outsourcing their editing?

Good editors are comfortable with sitting in front of a computer screen—and seeking to understand the POV of the person speaking and how it relates to the overall presentation and audience.

You want people to look good (or sound good) to themselves and others. A host or co-host who knows they'll be looked over with thoughtful consideration will be confident to give a more free performance, knowing someone has his or her back down the line.

Here's an insider tip for editing audio:

Besides the typical "waveform editing," which is seeing sound as drawing that increases or decreases in height and/or depth based on the volume (decibels, db) of the sound across a length of time, there's also "spectral editing." And it can be used alongside a traditional waveform. With spectral editing, sound shows up based on sound frequency (Hz, not volume) graph across a length of time.

Looking at a waveform versus spectral drawing will reveal different aspects of a sound recording and are helpful when used together to ensure you place your edits at "clean points" for smooth sound edits.

Content Rules

As the biggest podcast company in the world, Acast is a global leader in producing and monetizing content that matters. Director of Development Rebecca Steinberg took the time to answer a few questions for this book.

Bert: How important is content when you are choosing podcasts to join Acast?

Rebecca: It's incredibly important that the content we bring on aligns with our core values—that it's inclusive, of premium nature, well produced, and thoughtful. Scale is, of course, important from a sales perspective, but if the content doesn't speak to the Acast brand or help funnel new podcast listeners into the podcast space, we take a step back and make sure that we're taking on the content for the right reasons.

Bert: Is there a balance of content that Acast looks for when adding podcasts?

Rebecca: We're looking for all types of content—our goal is to be able to provide content to all listeners and meet them where they're at across all genres. We host shows that cover everything from health and wellness to beauty to reality TV to true crime to science and more.

Bert: What do you look for in podcast content?

> **Rebecca**: We're looking for authenticity and high production value—shows that reach a broad audience set and are dedicated to producing high-quality, thoughtful shows.

Set Yourself Free

Mark Podolsky is the self-proclaimed "Land Geek"—a guy who's figured out how to make millions by investing in real estate and now coaches others in the art of getting dirt rich. He has a pretty successful podcast, too, but I include him in this book because he's the King of Outsourcing. Mark whittled his actual working hours to about two per month by outsourcing everything from deeds to due diligence. This requires super-savvy delegation skills, which Mark has down to a science. At the core of what makes it work is that he records himself doing the task once and gives that video to the editor. Just start a Zoom call alone, share your screen, and talk through everything you're doing and why. Then outsource to a pro but give them the freedom to improve the process. The video gives them your thoughts and sensitivities—and being open to their suggestions gives them the freedom to improve things further using their expertise.

The Best of the Best

When it comes to feedback you must avoid one thing: *do not* ask your friends or family to listen to your podcast and give you help. You actually sought out the one person in the world more clueless than you for feedback! They are too close to you to give advice, and you are too close to them to listen to it constructively. Nothing good comes from this. Ever.

So where do you find someone with impeccable expertise in content and delivery—someone who can listen with a professional, tender ear and give you constructive feedback to take you to the next level? *My hand is raised!* At Pionaire Podcasting, I am the consultant to all our talent and I *love* this part of the job. I'll listen to your podcast and you and I can put a game plan together based on your strengths and unique personality to create a show that connects with your listeners by highlighting your content and delivery. I've focused my entire career on content and delivery, and I'm in the trenches every day, still creating both. I'd love to see if we're a good fit and bring your podcast to meet your goals. Hit me up at pionairepodcasting. com/consulting. I'm the adorable lil' guy on the home page. Some say dashing, even.

NOW HEAR THIS

- Know what you're strong at and know your weaknesses—where you need help. Then, hire the best and the people you trust to take over.
- Outsource to create new dollars because you can make more money by going deeper and building your brand.
- There is no shame in asking for help!

Part 3:
Your Plan

CHAPTER 6:

Showtime

Dax Shepard's *Armchair Expert* is "a podcast that celebrates the messiness of being human." His show, however, is anything but messy. It's carefully structured to welcome guests such as Justin Timberlake, Carey Mulligan, Tom Brady, and Randy Jackson with humor, candor, and authenticity. At the end of each show, Dax lists affiliates (with links on the Armchair Expert website related to content on the show or his own connections). Fight-Camp, HelloFresh, FIGS, and BetterHelp are just a few of the examples.

Armchair Expert's pace, banter, celebrity guests, and high-profile affiliates have made the podcast a success. So has its consistency—new episodes air Mondays and Thursdays—and each show lasts about ninety minutes. Listeners love this.

Earlier, I wrote about my mentor, Kidd Kraddick, and how he would come into the studio five minutes before the show with no schedule, write three things on a piece of paper, and ad-lib his way through four hours of the show. Every morning. I'm not that talented. And, no offense, my bet is neither are you.

You need a plan.

It's okay to break the rules sometimes if you have an extra-long episode or something like that. But as a new podcaster, you'll feel more comfortable with structure. It makes it easier for you to plan your show, but you don't have to stress if you're going a few minutes long on the first part.

With a plan, you can sound as if you had no plan and are just flowing through each interview flawlessly. So here's how you put your show together and keep your act together.

When to Publish Your Podcast

Big podcasts today don't necessarily have to worry about when they publish because they most likely have loyal listeners who will download the episode no matter what time it's available.

But what about if you're launching a new podcast?

Luke Riley, a data analyst at Megaphone, has done some research on podcasts and whether the timing of publication affects overall downloads. His research shows the most popular times to publish a podcast are Wednesdays at 2 a.m., Thursdays at 2 a.m., and Tuesdays at 11 p.m. Publishing midweek shows the most promise, as research reveals people tend to download the most on Tuesdays, Wednesdays, and Thursdays. This may be surprising, but the numbers of downloads decrease rapidly on the weekends.[17]

Why is it popular to publish so early? The theory is it beats the listener's morning commute. Many people listen to podcasts while they drive to work, and so it makes sense why the most popular time to publish podcasts is in the wee hours.

The podcasts that tend to get the most attention are published between the hours of 2 a.m. and 4 a.m. Avoid publishing from 11 p.m. to 1 a.m., when the number of downloads plummets.

Show Schedule

Mic: Check.
Co-hosts: Check.
Recording equipment: Check.

You've set up your studio with all these new mics, you and your co-hosts sit down ready to make the world's first podcast that goes from *zero* listeners to the top of the iTunes

---

17 Luke Riley, "Luke Riley: What Time Should You Publish Your Podcast?," RAIN News, May 9, 2019, https://rainnews.com/luke-riley-what-time-should-you-publish-your-podcast/.

podcast chart in *one* week. It's never been done before. But stand back, world, you're about to make history.

You start recording, open the mic and … *and* … *and* … everybody looks at each other with the expression of: "Well, who's gonna start? What are we gonna talk about?"

You were gonna *wing it?!* I'm laughing at you so hard that I'm doubled over in pain right now. Wing it? *Lol lol lol lol.*

Just. No.

Your show needs some kind of set schedule. Period. I know. I know. You have mad ad-libbing skills and you're the world's most gifted conversationalist. You still need to really think out a set schedule before you get in the studio. If you have co-hosts, you need to have a pre-planning meeting where everybody contributes content. This is no different from a bunch of writers on *Saturday Night Live* pitching their sketches. Not all of them make it on TV. Not all ideas make it on the podcast. So you have to formulate a hard schedule for everybody to follow. If you're doing your podcast solo, you still need to follow a schedule.

It might look something like this.

My Podcast Show Schedule

1. Intro: Welcome to (name of podcast).
2. One sentence mission statement: (Each week I/we _____.)

3. This week: Sensationalize tease of contents of show ("This week I talked to Gary V, and I can honestly say this conversation changed my life forever. He told me three things that make a company destined to fail, how to spot the best social media empires at the ground level, and the one relationship every successful entrepreneur has that sets them apart from all others.") Or: "This week is a game changer because I have proven science of the three elements that make any long-term marriage work. Astrologically, you'll know by the end of the show today if your relationship is doomed or not. And my bf snuck into my DMs and pretended to be another person and now I'm single."

4. Topic One: Three elements that make marriage work.

5. Tease: "I looked at this list of the three scientific elements of long-term relationships and I knew I was in trouble."

6. Content: The points you *must* make during this convo. Put the most important first!

7. *Tease Next Topic:* Doomed Astrologically. "Your relationship is doomed and you have no idea. It's because you're not aligned astrologically."

8. Content: Again, the points you *must* make during this convo. (Lather, rinse, repeat with the remaining podcast topics.)

9. Conclusion.

10. Tease next week's episode.

Of course, no single schedule fits all. Only you know if you're better with a lot of guidance or just a few notes that will spark convo. The point is you have to design some kind of schedule.

Here's an example from *In The Moement*.

In The Moement Podcast
Episode 53

Intro

- Farted during prayer

Things I'm Mad At

- My throat is embarrassing
- Thanks Moe, he's dead
- Credit cards
- Waiting at the movies

Shout Outs

- Man with seventeen kids
- Toilet man

Down to Business

- Kevin Hart
- Lauren London

Listen to Life?

- Tom Brady compares to life

Laugh of the Week

- I f&*^ed my hair up

Moement of the week

- Digging deep in your patience bag

Reflective Moement of the week

- I'm mad at how many years it took me to truly be myself

Quote of the Week
- Nipsey: You gotta be a beast

Tailoring to Your Audience

Remember how much we discussed your audience? Well, your show structure is a great opportunity to give them what they want. Even more specifically, consider how your audience can download content. Recently, I stumbled upon a post that mentioned *The Bert Show* as an example of a morning show podcast with individual episodes for each bit or segment.

"Many morning shows tend to upload their entire daily shows as single podcast episodes (such as Elvis Duran and the Morning Show)," wrote the poster. "However, I don't have time to listen to the entire thing. I prefer being able to download individual segments based on topics that interest me.

"My ideal example is The Bert Show, which is a nationally syndicated show based out of Atlanta. Every day, they upload individual episodes for each segment. Sometimes they are light hearted and funny, and other times it's more serious topics (spouse cheating, relationship advice, family drama, etc.). Each one is typically about 5–10 min. I would love to find another show like this."

Repeat after Me: Consistency

Consistency creates trust and builds momentum.

As a listener, I find nothing more maddening than when my fav podcast goes AWOL for a week with zero explanation. As a consultant, I think this is a huge breach of your relationship with your audience. You worked hard for your audience's loyalty. Don't take it for granted. And that's exactly what an inconsistent podcast does. Look, this podcasting thing is hard work. And there is *no* quicker way to lose an audience than by disrespecting them.

You must have a consistent delivery day and stick to it. I suggest that our talent have two or three podcasts saved for the weeks when "life happens." Ya know? Family emergencies, scheduling problems. Never miss a week of your podcast. *BROADly Speaking*, a podcast hosted by Davi Crimmins and Cassie Young, is doing something brilliant on this front. For the weeks Davi and Cassie are on vacation, they produce mini-podcasts to keep the audience engaged.

Full disclosure: my company, Pionaire Podcasting, consults for *BROADly Speaking*, and Cassie is also the Executive Vice President, Digital & Marketing of Pionaire Podcasting Network and *The Bert Show*. She's brilliant. And she's under contract, so don't even think about it! Her thoughts on mini episodes:

"The consistency of delivering your podcast is one thing. However, consistency in promoting and marketing your podcast is important too. At Pionaire Podcasting, we have a marketing schedule we construct with our talent to be sure they are marketing across social media at the right times to maximize their growth. There is pre-promotion, launch-day promotion, and post-promotion scheduled every week. We provide the schedule, and our talent provides the content. Sometimes it's audio samples of the podcast. Other's times it's the talent talking about what's coming up on this week's episode. But it's done consistently each week to build an audience. Which is so tough. You need every edge to get noticed. And consistency is a main ingredient."

The Beauty of Podcasting Is Editing

Remember Tiffany and Lauren from *Permission to Enter*? At first they put everything up, which listeners don't need or want. It's the same as when I'm doing a live show and our material just stinks. The beauty of podcasting is editing. You have to have an ear for it and take your ego out of it. Part of what made *Call Her Daddy* so popular were the hours and hours of editing that went into each show. They edited it down to their best content and their best conversations.

Earlier, I talked a bit about Ryan Dobson and how he and his wife have mastered the art of collaboration in their parenting podcast. But I also talked about Ryan's passionate belief in the power of high-quality content. If you need a reminder, "High quality is KING!"

There's a reason Ryan and his wife have found the success they have, and it goes beyond playing to each of their team members' strengths. Their podcast is reinforced heavily by the fact that they employ team members whose strengths specifically lie in beautiful editing. Ryan and Laura might speak the truth but, without the right editing, they might as well be as indecipherable as the static you'd see on a cable TV.

The Equipment You Need

Yes, you'll need a microphone, of course. But which kind? And what else? This will depend on your preferences and your podcast, and also on the ever-changing technology. As I write, however, these are the go-to items for anyone wishing to host a successful podcast. You can download even more information at pionairepodcasting.com.

- Microphone
- Windscreen
- Mic Stand
- Headphones
- Recording Software
- Audio Cleaning
- Hosting
- Show Artwork

The Secret Sauce

Breaking your podcast up into segments is the secret sauce that's going to get you paid.

One guy I know does a two-hour sports show in Jacksonville. I told him about chopping it up into segments. Jags fans who just want to hear about the Jags game average only about three thousand five hundred. But his overall listeners are up five hundred from him breaking the show up into segments.

When I take a look at my numbers every day, eight thousand people listen to the whole podcast or at least are downloading the whole podcast. Eight thousand. That means one hundred forty-two thousand of my downloads are coming from people checking out the segments—that's where the money is.

One podcaster who has a huge bottle of the secret sauce is John Lee Dumas of *Entrepreneurs on Fire*. He creates specific segments—and saves himself a boatload of time— by sending his guests questions (often the same questions about entrepreneurship) before they participate in the show. So during the interview, he can breeze through his part because the guests already know the questions and their answers. At one point, John had it scheduled so that every Friday, he was doing seven or eight 20-minute interviews in a row. He's making more than a million dollars a year, so it works. It's different from how I roll because I focus on the art of conversation and the connections we create—but he makes his approach very clear.

Another example can be found in Aryeh Sheinbein. I've told you all about his "Lion's Den Concept," but he also has made a (smart) habit of breaking the ice with his guests *before* they go on air. Building that chemistry and shattering any nerves means that not only does the conversation go more swimmingly but also that guests are able to dive into the juicy stuff sooner rather than later. There's no boring the listener with introductions. It's kind of like skipping the first day of class in high school. We can teleport past, "Hi, my name is Victoria and I love to juggle when I'm not eating Dutch pancakes." Instead, we'll dive into a deeper conversation with Victoria so she can bring the value we have her on the podcast for. Get it?

Planning Your Teases

A tease is a sensationalized line that gets your listener excited about your upcoming content. You want to use the 80/20 theory. You give them 80 percent of the story and they stick around for the other 20 percent because they are so intrigued. Here are some bad teases I've heard, along with my suggestions to make them much better.

Bad tease: You guys, I had the most awkward thing happen at my chiropractor's office.

Great tease: Guys, my chiropractor asked me if he could stick his finger up my rear during my appointment this week.

See the difference? Generally, when somebody tells you a story consists of a finger in the rear, you're going to stick around for the payoff. (Maybe that's just me.)

Bad tease: This week we're going to discuss the one thing most of you guys are doing wrong when training your dog.

Good tease: I know two clients who were sued by neighbors because they made the same mistake 90 percent of dog owners make when training their dogs.

When you hear statistics along with a little legal drama, you're more likely to tune in for that podcast, right?

Three Ways to Tease during Your Podcast

Table-of-contents tease: You have a podcast with a series of great topics you're going to discuss during your episode. Consider teasing the three most intriguing stories; it's like offering a table of contents. No matter how many "segments" you have time to include, you want listeners sticking around because they can't miss the three you teased in the beginning of your podcast. Here's an example from one of my shows:

"So much to cover this week.

- Moe's sister is lucky to be alive this week. She literally struggled for her life while a guy tried to kidnap her on a college campus.
- My mom has dementia and is not fit to continue being a therapist, but she still desperately wants to continue her practice. Is it ethical for me to hire actors for her to counsel so she thinks she's still working?
- I know a dude who slept with a woman during a trial separation from his wife. She walked right in on him in their own home! She says he was cheating. He says, no way. Who's right?"

In this example, I used that 80/20 rule. My listeners know the root of the content, but they'll want to stick around for the other 20 percent.

I might get to four other things in our show. But I want listeners intrigued enough to wait for those top-of-the-podcast, table-of-contents teases.

If you're focusing on one topic during your podcast, be sure to give your audience reasons to stick around and the feeling that they are going to miss something big if they leave you: "You are wasting your time on 95 percent of investment websites. I have five that have never given me bad advice."

Immediately tease the best content on your podcast—even before you sell those endorsements (wink). Listeners will hear the moneymaking aspects of your show when you've got them hooked with table-of-contents teases.

Transition teases: Following the same 80/20 formula, use a tease from one topic to the other. Avoid rookie-sounding transitional teases such as "Moving on," "So that's how that ended," and "So let's take a look at _____ now." The world has zero need for those. Once you're done with a topic, let the momentum pause. Take a breath. Then launch right into the tease to make sure they hang out for the next segment. It will feel strange the first couple of times, and you may fail at keeping it smooth, but I assure you no listener is thinking: "Man, give me a transitional line or something before starting your next story. I'm never listening again. This person is terrible at transitioning. Loser. I'm giving them a one-star rating because of their awful transitions. A person who can't transition is so unlovable."

Let's go back to the sample show I included above. These were the transition teases:

"So they caught that monster, my sister won't leave her apartment and my dad has moved in with her. It's a total cluster, but we're lucky she's alive." (Pause, breath.) "My mom would have no idea if I hired an actor to play the part of a new patient because my mom has dementia. So, why would I even consider doing this …?"

You'll use the same formula with each and every transition into a new topic. The smart play is to write these down on your show schedule to use as a reference when switching topics. (You're thinking: "Whoa. Wait? Did this dude just write 'show schedule?' What the heck? Now I have to do a show schedule?" Indeed. But more on that in a bit.)

Remember, when you're editing your show, leave in spaces between transitions instead of immediately cutting out the sound of your breath. Choppy edits that eliminate your natural breath sound awkward. You want them to sound natural.

End-of-episode teases: You have just completed your hall-of-fame episode. Nobody in the history of podcasts has provided the kind of entertaining insight that you just did. Your audience laughed. They cried. Their hearts sang and you touched the depths of their soul in a way no podcaster ever has. They experienced unimaginable joy and discovered the meaning of life. So now what? Make sure they know that your next episode is going to be equally epic. How? You need to have one or two things to tease for your next episode. Use that 80/20 rule the same way.

- "Next Tuesday when I drop the next episode, I'll tell ya about walking into my parents' bedroom to find my mom in a swing with my eighty-two-year-old father. Don't forget to subscribe …"

- "I didn't get to it this week, but in my next podcast on Thursday, I promise to tell you guys the three beauty secrets that every celebrity uses in their press photos that will immediately upgrade your online presence."

- "I recorded a conversation with the one and only Gary V last week. I can't believe I got the interview. But he told me two things about getting started in business that changed my life and it will change yours too. That's on Monday. Do *not* miss that one."

Your teases *must* be sensationalized. You want to make your listener eager to get to next week's episode. *Then* you have to tease that episode all week long on social media or marketing. *Wait, what?!* You weren't expecting that, right? *Teasing all week on social? Marketing?*

When you tease on social, be sure to sensationalize the same way. For example:

- Bad social tease: "The one and only Gary V joins me on Tuesday's podcast."

- Good social tease: "The world's premier entrepreneur, Gary V, joins me to tell you the three elements of starting a business or it's destined to fail."

(OMG. That interview didn't even happen and I'm excited to listen to that made-up podcast!)

🎧 NOW HEAR THIS

- With a plan, you can sound as if you had no plan and are just flowing through each interview flawlessly.
- Your show needs some kind of set schedule. Period!
- A tease is a sensationalized line that gets your listener excited about your upcoming content. You want to use the 80/20 theory. You give them 80 percent of the story and they stick around for the other 20 percent because they are so intrigued.
- Consider teasing the three most intriguing stories; it's like offering a table of contents.

CHAPTER 7:

Interview Secrets

I've had great interviews. I've had awful interviews. Every bad interview I ever did was because the guest sucked. I was always fantastic.

I'm joking, of course. As a general rule, I've found that the interview is only as good as the guest. If your guest is closed, the interview will suck. If the guest isn't a conversationalist, the interview will suck. If the guest would rather be somewhere else, the interview will suck.

Chris Rock was a terrible interview. But I blame this on his booking agent. He was promoting a movie and clearly didn't want to be hanging out with me. He wasn't funny. And when I asked if he feels pressure to be funny all the time, he looked at me and said: "Well, I turn it on when I have to. Like, I'm going on *Oprah* in a few weeks. I'll turn it on then."

We were the first show in the country to interview Justin Bieber. He trusts us, so we have a familiarity in our interviews now. They're *always* good.

Howard Stern's interviews are always great because he's built a brand around the fact that anybody who walks into his studio is required to answer *every one* of his provocative questions. To his credit, he's earned that!

Having the solid foundation I've set you up for so far allows you to attract potentially provocative interviews yourself. So here's how to make the most of them.

Keep the Interviews Evergreen

Tom Schwab of Interview Valet points out the evergreen nature of interviews on podcasts; people can listen to them anytime. So if you spend an entire interview discussing this year's Super Bowl, it will be irrelevant in a matter of days. "Talk about things that an expert would know," he says. "The best podcast content that a guest can give is interesting ideas and things that will cause people to question and talk about it. A podcast going viral means that I listen to a podcast and then the rest of the day start talking about it and say, 'You know, I was listening to a podcast this morning and the host was talking about this idea. I've never thought about it that way.' That's the amazing part where it goes from just being in a podcast to being talked about throughout the day." This means including bigger ideas and timeless content a listener would only learn through your podcast.

Everybody Wins

"We always tell the guest that your goal for being on the show is to make the hosts look like a genius for introducing you," says Tom. "You should be there to serve because if you do a good job serving, they will promote you better than you ever could because if you start promoting yourself, you sound vain. But if you do a good job, the host will promote you better than you ever could."

Podcasters should never ruin their authority or their relationship with their guest, adds Tom. "So every interview should be a win for everybody," he says. "It should be a win for the audience first, the host second, and the podcast guest third. And all of those have to win or it doesn't make sense. One of the things that we always teach our clients is before the interview, the best question to ask the host is, what are you hoping to get out of this interview? What can I do to serve you and your audience? Begin with the end in mind, as Stephen Covey would say. It's great because the guest will tell you what her audience is like, what means most to them. Content is king, but context is god. They'll tell you where they want to go. And most people are nice. So if you ask what the guest is hoping to get out of the interview, chances are they'll ask the same question of you."

Do Your Homework

Don't get enamored by the name of the guest. Do your homework. I interviewed Harrison Ford. Good God, almighty. I still have nightmares about it. Wonderful, talented actor. Probably a good guy. I wanted Indiana Jones to rock the mic. But he's a *suuuuuuper* slow talker. Monotone as hell. And boring. I don't wanna sound mean. I really don't. But I was enamored by having freaking Harrison Ford—Han Solo!—on the radio. I should have gone online and watched and listened to Harrison Ford in an interview setting. I didn't. That was the last time I ever did that.

I had Kevin James on the show three times. He was terrible the first time. I couldn't believe that Kevin James, from *The King of Queens*, was not funny. I figured he was having a bad day. So I booked him again. Same thing. I refused to believe it. CBS called and I booked him again in utter disbelief that Kevin James wasn't funny 24/7. Same results. Maybe it was my questions? Maybe Kevin James hates radio interviews but was forced to do them? I don't know. The point is I should have done my research. I should have listened to him on other shows and made a decision to have him on my show based on quality, not ego. While writing this book, I received a call from Netflix requesting an interview with Kevin James. *I took the interview.* But a scheduling conflict occurred right before the interview took place. To this day I refuse to believe Kevin James is a bad interview.

Let's take out the celebrity portion of this. This principle is similar for any interview. Chances are pretty good you won't be the first interview this guest has ever done. Watch, listen, and read their previous interviews. Are they vulnerable? Do they share? Are they good conversationalists? Are they interesting? Do they communicate effectively? Will they allow you to be a good interviewer? Will your audience walk away feeling good about you based on the interview?

Know what you're getting into. Look, you're online stalking your first date before you go out, right? ("Awwww … look at all the pictures with puppies, he has marriage potential." "Whoa, she looks amazing in a pair of Lululemons, she has marriage potential.") So, why would you not use the same stalker intelligence on someone you're going to interview? Is he worth your time? Does she seem interesting?

You know why Joe Rogan is a great interviewer? It's super clear that he knows his stuff. So many guests. So many topics. It's so evident the dude is educated on every topic and intimately knows his guests. And they immediately respect him because he respects them by knowing his stuff. I don't know whether he does the homework himself or whether he has producers that do most of the leg work. I guess it doesn't matter. Either way, I have never heard him caught off guard in an interview because he's so well-schooled.

Apply the same technique to your interviews. I can't tell you how many hours that is. But every time I've done a big interview, I've spent hours on homework. I want to feel secure that I know the guests and thoroughly know their material. Most of the time, I've done so much homework I feel I know the guest so well that I know how they will respond before I ask the question. I know their personality. I know their history. I could play them in a movie.

Lewis Howes is one of the great podcasting interviewers. His podcast, *The School of Greatness*, focuses on interviewing hundreds of top-notch personalities who consistently have incredible insight into how to live a happy life. He told me he spends a couple of hours doing homework on each guest. The end result might be a sixty-minute podcast, but he'll spend two to three times that long on researching his guest.

Conversely, I've done too much research on a guest and felt determined to get to every question because I put so much time into the homework. I never heard the guests' answers because I was so focused on getting to all my questions. For example, I had a forty-five-minute interview with Lady Gaga that people tell me was good. But I have no idea because I didn't listen to her answers. I just sped through the interview like Usain Bolt never listening or asking follow-up questions.

For all I know, the interview went like this:

Lady Gaga: "I just got back from a trip to the moon, where I performed 'Born This Way' with the ghost of Neil Armstrong."

Me: "Cool. How was it kissing Bradley Cooper in that movie you did with him?"

Focus on the First Two Minutes

It's essential to set the tone for the entire interview in the first few minutes. The guest is assessing if this is an environment they feel safe in immediately. If they don't feel safe, you are in trouble. They'll be closed and you'll never get a great interview if you mess this up initially. So you know how I combat that? Kiss their butt. Like hard. Like enough where you're super close to leaving a butt hickey. They need to know you're a fan. Again, they gotta feel safe. They have to feel you're coming from a good place. Most guests are insecure about being ambushed or not being capable of answering your questions. Put their minds at ease that you're an ally.

Let Your Guest Be the Star

Is there anything more annoying than listening to an interviewer try to out-expert the expert? Your job is to get the best out of your guest—not to prove to the guest that you know as much as they do. Telling Stephen Hawking you know the difference between the Big Dipper and Little Dipper as well as he does will do nothing for your interview. Your job is to move the interview forward by being genuinely inquisitive and always keeping the interest of your audience as your motivation. How is this interview bettering your listener? Is it entertaining for them? You can learn along the way too. But that's the secondary motivation.

Interview People You're Genuinely Interested In

Ed Mylett, peak performance expert, is giddy over the guests he brings on to his podcast. His energy and excitement are contagious. He can't wait to ask questions that will better him and his audience. You genuinely feel he's so excited to help his audience with each and every answer his guest provides. This can only be done if you respect and are excited about your guest.

In my past interviews, you could clearly hear the difference between my interest level interviewing J. Lo and my interest level interviewing Mike Sorrentino from Jersey Shore. You cannot hide authenticity. And if you have no interest in your guest, your audience will feel it.

Killer interviews will make or break your podcast. But you can do more to get people to really love you, which we'll discuss in the next chapter.

NOW HEAR THIS

- The best podcast content that a guest can give is interesting ideas and things that will cause people to question and talk about it.
- It's essential to set the tone for the entire interview in the first few minutes.
- Do your homework—hours of homework—for each and every guest.
- Interview people who genuinely interest you.
- Do not ever try to out-expert the expert you're interviewing.

CHAPTER 8:

Building a Cult Following

I like to think I have a cult following (doesn't everybody?). But seriously, I have an incredibly loyal audience that's been spreading the word about *The Bert Show* to more and more listeners every day. This has come from 100 percent authenticity and vulnerability, which built trust when we first started *The Bert Show*.

We were on a brand new signal—three thousand watts—and we were going up against fifty thousand-watt radio stations. The very first day, I went on the air and said, "Look, I've been doing radio for ten or fifteen years and I'm super scared to host my own show. I'm not exactly sure what to do—bear with us through the construction of it. We're going to have a pretty good product. But I can't promise you anything for the next couple of months."

Everybody on the show was in a new role, and I had never hosted a show. My co-host on the show was more of a behind-the-scenes producer guy, so it was a new role for him too. Plus, we had a reality TV star who had never done radio. We were all brand new, and I was just 100 percent honest, saying, "We don't know what we're doing."

From that authenticity, it grew and grew and grew to where people trusted us. When you're building a cult following, it's all about connecting and people feeling that they trust you and they feel safe with you. It all starts from there.

This chapter will walk you through the final instructions for building a podcast that lasts and lasts, which includes doing good in the world, getting emotional, and rewarding fans, as well as more insider tips from the top.

Add the Emotional Details

The emotional detail and connection to the backstory make it a way more intimate experience for a listener.

Emotional detail is so much more powerful than physical detail. Both are hard to do well. Being vulnerable and connecting emotionally to the material you're delivering is what separates good communicators from great communicators.

The beauty of nonvisual entertainment is that you get to paint pictures with your words. It's unlike any other platform. We can describe in vivid color what a scene looks like, which is a talent in itself. Adding emotion to the scene gives your conversation life and relatability.

So many put too much focus on the physical parts of storytelling and miss diving into the most important emotional parts that make an audience feel like they are part of the experience.

Remember Kristin Ingram? We talked about her podcast for fellow mothers, and there's a reason she's all about embracing emotionality with her listeners. While Kristin might not have an enormous following, she definitely has a loyal following—and her listeners are loyal largely because they see her as a friend, not a face. Kristin never spares her own emotional details, and she's willing to wear her heart on her sleeve when she responds to her listeners. She's a prime example of how you can help your audience to feel like they're participants whom you care deeply about.

It doesn't matter what your podcast is about—the center of the podcast will be you as the content deliverer. There are thousands of podcasts that focus on money and finances. What is your life experience to share and connect with the audience on the topic of finances? What were your personal highs and lows in the industry that connect you with your audience? Why are you in the financial game? What was your motivation? What makes me want to cheer for you and follow you?

Reward and Prioritize Fans

Tony Robbins and Taylor Swift are just two examples of celebrities who are brilliant at building a cult following by catering to their fans. But you don't need to go to great lengths in order to make your listeners feel special. At *The*

Bert Show, we've hosted what we call "P1" parties for our most hard-core fans. Every Friday, we bring in twelve to fifteen listeners, who get to sit in the studio while we're doing the show. If any of them have an interesting story, I'll put them on the air. We give away gift certificates.

So identify your most rabid fans—you can do this through analytics—and reward them. It's as simple as that. For an example of rewarding rabid fans, look at how Pabst Blue Ribbon (PBR) has tapped into community influencers. When *The Real World* debuted, Puck gave us a glimpse into the world of bike messengers, an underground group of influencers at the time. PBR focused just on those bike messengers and started to give them PBR gear. Then, as PBR became the go-to beer at dive bars, they gave people free PBR at dive bars. This was all with zero marketing dollars. It's about using that same understanding of human psychology with your most loyal listeners and then embracing them, rewarding them, and recognizing them.

I'll never forget when I sent a message to one of my favorite podcasters, Ed Mylett, and he called me back and left a voice mail. Hearing his voice—a voice I listen to all the time on his podcast—energized me so much. I felt special. As podcasters, you can make people feel special,

When it comes to recognizing fans, I also respond directly on social media—99.9 percent of the comments and messages get a personal reply from me. All it takes is five seconds to write "Thanks for listening," or "I agree," or even just a simple thumbs up. People share this with their friends and family members, increasing that cult following.

And I ignore the haters, as I mentioned earlier in this book. It's a sign that you've made it because they can't hate you if they don't know you just as they can't love you if they don't know you. I say this to my staff all the time because some of those nasty comments can hurt. And I say to them, in any given fifteen minutes, we have about fifteen thousand people who are checking us out. If we were doing the show on a stage in a stadium and there were fifteen thousand people there and five of those fifteen thousand walked out of our show and hated us, would we even notice them? Would we even pay attention to them? The truth of the matter is absolutely not. Five out of fifteen thousand. The percentages are in your favor.

Fifteen Ways to Grow Your Podcast to Ten Thousand Downloads or More, from Neil Patel

1. Begin with value before you ever launch
2. Produce quality audio without the cost
3. Find the super listeners
4. Find guests who fit your niche
5. Brand with clarity
6. Be everywhere your audience downloads content
7. Hack to the top of Apple's "New & Noteworthy"
8. Friend of a friend
9. Contribute to the tribe
10. Leverage your social network
11. Inspire your audience to take action

12. Show up again and again and again
13. Improve your interviewing skills with practice
14. Interview swap
15. Get ranked in search[18]

Connecting Is the Key

I've written about this earlier in the book, and I'm writing about it again because connection is sincerely important. Huge. Ginormous. (I can't believe that word made it past spell check.) Immense. Massive. Colossal. Connecting with an audience is the key to being loved by an audience. Not liked. Loved. And love is where the money is.

In order to truly connect, you have to share. What makes you endearing to your audience? What makes them want to follow you? What makes them cheer for you?

My parents were the worst parents ever. Both narcissistic. Both dismissive. Once I was born, they felt their job was kinda done. My therapist told me it's an absolute act of God I didn't end up more dysfunctional than I did. Now I have a tough time connecting on an intimate level. It takes me forever to trust a new person in my circle.

They told me when I was three years old that I'd never write a book about podcasting. Okay, they never told me that. In fact, there was no podcasting when I was three. The point is that I had no problem sharing any of my

---

18   Neil Patel, "Hack Your Way to 10,000 Podcast Downloads with These 15 Tips," Neil Patel, April 22, 2018, https://neilpatel.com/blog/grow-your-podcast/.

upbringing during my morning show. And it connected me with other dysfunctional listeners.

So what is connecting you? Anybody can give info on taxes, relationships, green beans, technology, meditating, sloths, exotic vacations, whatever. The difference is connecting yourself with those topics through vulnerability, realness, or trust that sets you apart from the other podcasts focusing on the same subject.

How are you going to intimately connect? Are you brave enough to do that? This takes real courage!

There is a huge difference between talking and connecting. I once had a member of my team say: "People love us. They want to hear all about us no matter what we're doing." *No! Just, no!* Just because you're you and just because you're talking doesn't make you entertaining. And this is a big mistake I hear podcasters making. Is your ego getting in the way of knowing what's really interesting? Listeners have a bazillion podcasts to listen to now. So what's making some successful? Connection. Pure and simple. Anybody can give out advice. Anybody can provide detailed information. But how are you connecting to the material on a more intimate level? On a personal level. What is unique about your voice? What are you brave enough to share that others won't? What can you communicate for people to love you?

Again, Make It Evergreen

Two of the longest-running podcasts are *Podrunner* and *Groovelectric*, both founded in 2006 by California's

DJ Steve Boyett. "I was the first kid on the block," says Steve, who was coaxed by his aerobics-teacher girlfriend to create playlists designed for working out. He was one of the early gods of podcasting. His mixes soon landed atop the iTunes chart, and Steve was getting six hundred thousand downloads per month—a big milestone back in the dinosaur days of podcasting.

Today, millions of people continue to tune into *Podrunner* and *Groovelectric*, as Steve's learned to make a living off simply doing what he loves best: mixing funky jams. He takes no advertising; refuses to be part of Facebook, Instagram, or any social media; and marketing is only by word of mouth. How has he become such a massive success with a cult following of runners, walkers, dancers, office workers, and more? People love the music. "People aren't following me because they love my voice," he says. "I talk for two minutes. My relationship with the audience is not in the podcast; it's peripheral to it. I'm not part of the cult of personality, like Joe Rogan." But as he points out, his content is evergreen: the mixes he made in 2006 are just as relevant as those he releases fifteen years later.

"I accidentally got really popular, and I wasn't up against two million people when I started," says Steve, one of the co-chairs of the San Francisco Podcast Association." His tips for podcasters? "Have more desire than is reasonable to do it," says Steve. "And you need to have a discoverable, interesting, and relatively narrow niche." His third, and most important, tip is to educate yourself (which, of course, is what this book is doing for you), get some half-decent equipment, and sound good. You need to have some perspective on yourself and how you talk, how you sound, what your image is, how you come across, how focused you are," says Steve.

Do Good in the World

The role of doing good is a big component of building a cult following. Take a look at Dave Portnoy, the founder of Barstool Sports, who has connected with his podcast audience and is now building even more of a cult following with the small-business fund that has raised nearly thirty million dollars. He's taken a really hard stand for the little guy on Wall Street. When they have somebody champion their cause that they trust, that's where the following comes from. They are willing to follow you if they believe in you as an authentic, safe, trustworthy figure.

I have a nonprofit, called Bert's Big Adventure, that takes kids who have chronic and terminal illnesses to Disney World for a weekend every year. We bring everybody in the house and my listeners pay for the entire trip. In retrospect, the appeal for me to start this kind of trip was that my parents never took me on one family vacation. They just didn't think it was important. So I grew up without the memories or pictures of family trips. No laughter together; no reminiscing later in life about shared experiences. I was so jealous of my friends who would leave for a week at a time and come home with amazing stories about their family travels. I just didn't want kids to feel that kind of emptiness. So, now, taking financially challenged families to escape the everyday, stressful life that medically fragile kids live has filled my soul.

My listeners are really into Bert's Big Adventure. I built this by going on the air and saying: "This is where my heart is. I want to take these kids down to Disney World. I want them to escape hospitals. I want them to escape doctors. I want them to escape syringes. I want to go down there for five days. I want to pay for the entire trip. And when I say, 'I,' I mean you guys. So there's the idea. Now, here's the kicker, you guys, I have no idea what I'm doing. I don't have anybody on staff who knows how to start something like this. I've never done a nonprofit. That's the idea. Who can help out?"

Phone call after phone call came in (I'd put them on the air) from people who were immediately ready to help and volunteer.

We started Bert's Big Adventure in 2002, and it became an organic experience that everybody embraced because my heart was in the right place. I connected on something that people believe in. Walt Disney World is built into the fabric of America. Almost every kid wants that experience. Since 2002, we've been bringing kids to see Cinderella's castle in person, to ride Space Mountain, and to walk down that magical Main Street. Sure, we've been down, money-wise some years. And I'll say: "Guys, here is the true situation. We need more donations." Suddenly, $50,000 comes in. My listeners have just embraced it because they believe in it. They believe in me, and they've connected with the cause. If you want to build a cult following, authenticity and integrity are where it starts.

Stay Patient

How long will it take you to build a cult following? We live in a world of instant gratification, and it's not going to happen overnight. I'm a big fan of a slow build. If you become really popular really quickly, some people may mistrust your genuine connection with your audience. I'd rather build a relationship and build my audience slowly rather than having this quick explosion of listeners or people who are sampling you right off the bat. And remember, a cult following can just be twenty people.

To bring back up the example of Dan Miller, he made this mistake himself. When he was starting to gain a podcast following in the 2001–2006 era, he thought radio was out the door. He was sure that there wasn't much popularity to be gained on that front, and that podcasting would become an outdated fad. He's the first to admit, in hindsight, that he should've been more patient. As he put it, "I should have stuck my feet in the sand."

You'll know by the numbers, sure; anytime I crack a mic, I can look at the analytics and see what's been working great for the audience. But for the cult following, it's more visceral. I could feel it when I started Bert's Big Adventure, and workers from Home Depot were calling in to help, along with listeners ready to send a check for $30,000. Even before I saw the numbers, I could feel it in my gut.

I want to repeat this. *Be patient.* Podcasting is *work.* A lot of work. You will not see instant results. I know celebrities who have been super frustrated because the numbers of their podcasts weren't paying big dividends within the first few months of their launch. *It takes time! A lot of time and work!* Do not get into podcasting expecting to be an overnight sensation. Unless you have a loyal following that is transferring over into your podcast, this is a painstakingly slow process.

NOW HEAR THIS

- The emotional detail and connection to the backstory make it a way more intimate experience for a listener.
- In order to truly connect, you have to share. What makes you endearing to your audience? What makes them want to follow you? What makes them cheer for you?
- Do good in the world.
- Focus on the quality of your cult following, not the quantity.
- *Be patient!*

CONCLUSION

Well, here we are. End of book. Your podcasting pad-awan training is now over. Jedi time!

Or is it?

Let's take a look into your future. Think of this as a "choose your own adventure."

Scenario A

You read everything in this book. And didn't apply anything.

You went out and got yourself the highest-rated microphone you could.

You built the Taj Mahal of podcasting studios, and you recorded your first podcast.

It was so good you didn't need an editor! It was eight hours long. Zero editing. You focused on twenty-seven topics ranging from the proper fertilizer to make your back lawn look marvelous and theories of QAnon to American Girl dolls and the failure of the XFL.

You did nine interviews and didn't research any of them and just allowed God to work through you.

You posted your podcast, shared it with both of your followers on Instagram, and nobody listened.

Clearly they didn't understand your genius.

You doubled down the next week and the next week and the next week: one hundred thirty hours of prime podcasting gold. You got a few friends and family to listen. They said they loved it, but they also laughed and ridiculed you.

Your mom stopped taking your calls.

Your dad wrote you out of his will.

Your friends muted you on social media.

You became a depressed recluse, toured the country in a renovated Geo Metro selling your plasma for income.

Sad. So very sad.

Scenario B

You read, absorbed, and executed *all* the key points of this book.

You pinpointed your audience and made a mission statement that delivered content each week with laser focus.

You got over your insecurities and started your podcast ugly. Slowly.

You hated your own voice, but you forged on.

You were patient and started with a mini podcast.

You drew in your audience quickly with enticing teases and outlined your show, delivering only the A material. You researched and built an amazing marketing strategy.

You identified super talented people and outsourced and used them for their expertise in areas you are clueless about.

You did your homework about the business of podcasting and monetized talent.

You are OCD-like consistent in delivering your podcast each and every week on the same day.

You connect and reward your most loyal fans.

And look at you now! Peaceful as Buddha, rich as Jeff Bezos, and celebrated like a prom king or queen, or both. You are content and fulfilled, and random strangers high five you as you walk down the street.

You have a fleet of shiny new cars, your own plane, dating the most internally and externally beautiful people.

From time to time, you find yourself the center of an unscripted yet flawlessly performing flash mob.

People want to be with you and want to be just like you.

You are content. You are whole. You are fulfilled.

Your parents are proud. Your grandmother makes you baked goods each week. You walk with pride and strangers wonder, "Who is that marvelous person?"

In a few words: you have it all. Just because you executed the blueprint of this book.

You. Are. Welcome.

Sincerely, I hope you get endless fulfillment out of your podcast. I hope you give yourself a lot of grace to make mistakes, learn from them, and move on. I hope you are patient because podcasting can be so liberating and fun and lucrative.

Enjoy your journey creating and finding your unique voice.

ACKNOWLEDGMENTS

Quite honestly, every person and every experience I've had doing a radio show or managing content should get some credit.

Jack Diamond introduced me to radio morning shows, and Kidd Kraddick was instrumental in teaching me to have zero boundaries and take risks. Mark Renier and Brian Philips hired me as an inexperienced host in Atlanta. Brian gave me the freedom to learn and create without fear.

Anybody who's contributed in a positive way to *The Bert Show* deserves acknowledgment. I have learned from each and every person that has been in the studio in one way or another. For those who were loyal and determined to create something special and matched (in some cases surpassed) my devotion to creating something legendary, thank you. Thank you, Tracey Kinney, Tommy Owen, and Kristin Klingshirn for your loyalty, patience, guidance, and integrity.

Everybody needs a team of trusted and loyal friends who are willing to give you tough love when you need it.

Sidney Poitier wrote, "When you go for a walk with some-one, something interesting happens unconsciously, either they adjust to your pace or you adjust to their pace." Assess your friends and ask yourself, are those relationships help-ful and healthy for you? No truer statement can be applied to a group of eight men I lean on because they make me keep up with their pace. I was lucky enough to be invited into this group of exceptional men who guide me emo-tionally and professionally. Without these dudes for sure this book would have never been written. Thank you to Quincy Jones for inviting me into this group of men who have made me a better man on so many levels: Chris Tuff, Tommy Breedlove, Taylor Barnes, Mike Domenicone, Hank McLarty, Marc Hodulich, and Peter Boulden.

My fiancée (maybe we'll be married by the time this book is done?), Tiffany Haynes, for always giving me the space to be creative and the gentle guidance and support this insecure guy needs from time to time.

Thank you, Chris Tuff, for making me think bigger than I ever could have imagined and guiding me through the next professional chapter of my life. And Sarah Tuff, Ethan Webb, Catherine Turner, and Nick Pavlidis, who patiently guided me through this book writing process.

Thank you Amy Howard, for your loyalty, support, and your exhaustive efforts to keep me organized.

Thank you to all the amazing people who agreed to be interviewed for the book.

Finally, thank you to my publisher, Morgan James Publishing, for helping me bring this book to life and giving me the guidance and freedom to produce a book I am excited to share with the world.

ABOUT THE AUTHOR

Bert Weiss was born in Brooklyn and began his professional career at a country radio station in San Diego as a research assistant. After inventing his own job title as Sports Director, he followed legendary personality Jack Diamond to Washington, DC, and ultimately landed in Atlanta in March 2001.

For the past twenty years, Bert has been entertaining audiences worldwide from this Atlanta base. *The Bert Show* now has one million listeners tuning in to the four-hour program each week. Bert and fellow cast members share life stories including struggles, triumphs, and all of the emotion in between. Bert also runs a nonprofit called Bert's Big Adventure, which takes children with chronic and terminal illnesses to Disney World for an all-expenses-paid, five-day trip with their families, and arranges regular reunions.

Most recently, Bert launched Pionaire, a podcasting talent network. When he's not on the radio, working on the show, or consulting, he's most likely found spending time with his family, traveling, or staying fit. Bert has two sons, Hollis and Hayden, and is engaged to be married to Tiffany Haynes, who has a daughter, Elizah. Some of his best travel memories include swimming freely with sea lions in the Galápagos, scaling the Via Ferrata in Telluride, Colorado, driving buggies on the beach in Brazil, and stargazing all night in Bora Bora.

A free ebook edition is available with the purchase of this book.

To claim your free ebook edition:

1. Visit MorganJamesBOGO.com
2. Sign your name CLEARLY in the space
3. Complete the form and submit a photo of the entire copyright page
4. You or your friend can download the ebook to your preferred device

Print & Digital Together Forever.

Snap a photo   Free ebook   Read anywhere